VOYAGES

RESEARCH-BASED MATHEMATICS

EXCURSIONS

Developed by
Metropolitan Teaching and Learning Company
and
The School District of Hillsborough County

SENIOR AUTHORS
AL SORIANO, JACK BEERS

Senior Authors
Albert Soriano, Jr.
Supervisor, Elementary Mathematics (retired)
School District of Hillsborough County

Jack Beers
Vice President, Math and Science
Metropolitan Teaching and
Learning Company

Author, K–5; Program Manager, K–2
Janet White
Elementary Mathematics
School District of Hillsborough County

Author, K–5; Program Manager, 3–5
John Fahle
Elementary Mathematics
School District of Hillsborough County

Author, K–5; Technical Design Manager, K–5
Keith Aborn
Elementary Mathematics
School District of Hillsborough County

Author, K–5; Lead Kindergarten Consultant
Barbara Knox
Elementary Mathematics
School District of Hillsborough County

Authors, School District of Hillsborough County
Todd Connolly
Lia Crawford
Gaye Katulich
Scott Weaver

Contributing Authors/Editors, School District of Hillsborough County
Johnny Biggens
Jill Bucholtz
Stephanie Clark
Mark Dunn
Jeffrey Guerra
Toynita Martinez
John Perry
Susan Rakes
Carol Skelton
Dorothy Trapnell

Contributing Resource Teachers, Elementary Mathematics, School District of Hillsborough County
Rita Dugan
Elizabeth Glenn (retired)

Design: Debrah Welling
Cover: Charles Yuen

Published by Metropolitan Teaching and Learning Company.
Printed in the United States of America.

Metropolitan Teaching and Learning Company
33 Irving Place
New York, NY 10003

ISBN 1-58830-628-3
3 4 5 6 DBH 10 09 08 07

Table of Contents

TOPIC 4:

TOPIC 5:

TOPIC 6:

TOPIC 7:

TOPIC 1

Data Collection and Analysis

Name ______________________________

A Picture Is Worth a Thousand . . .

THE KEY TO PICTOGRAPHS

1. The chart below shows the number of CDs (compact discs) that each student has in his or her music collection.

Name	Number of CDs
Jarred	40
Adriana	35
Brett	50
Keisha	70

Jarred wants to display this information by using a pictograph.

He is going to use this picture  to make his pictograph.

How many CDs should each  stand for? Explain your reasoning.

Complete the key and the pictograph below.

____

Key:  =

Use the pictograph below to answer questions 2–5.

Money Earned Doing Chores (September)

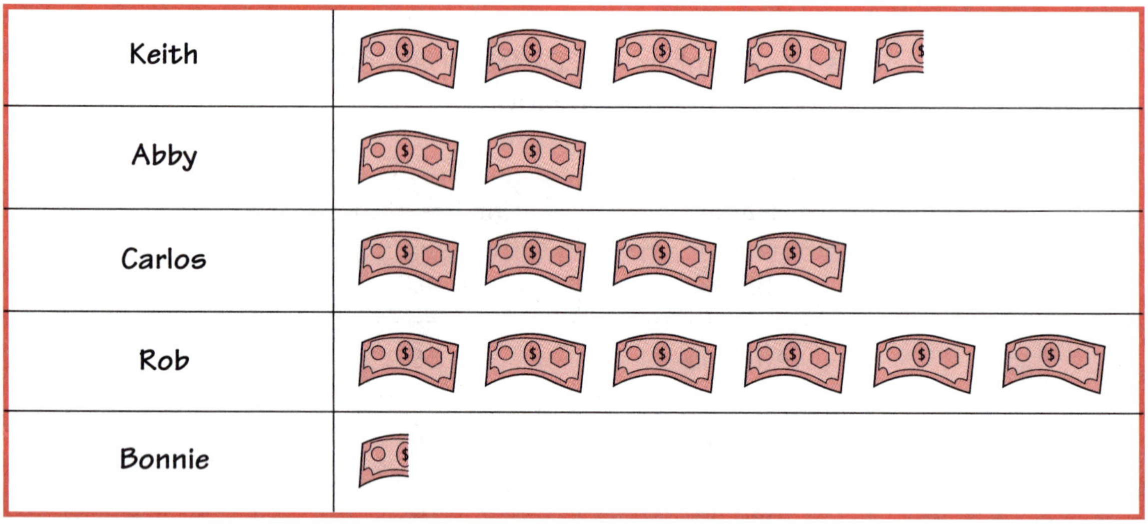

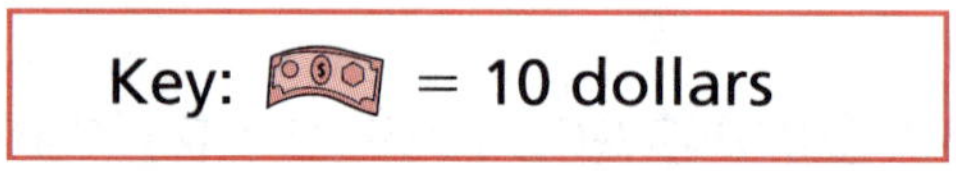

2. How much money did Keith earn in September?

3. Abby earned 20 dollars. Who earned twice as much as Abby?

4. Rob hoped to earn 100 dollars in the month of September. By how many dollars did Rob miss his goal?

5. One of the people broke an arm and was unable to do much work during the month of September. Which person might this be? Explain your reasoning.

Name ______________________________

SELL, SELL, SELL PICTOGRAPH

____

Key:

FUND-RAISING QUESTIONS

First Grade:

1. Of which two items did first graders sell the same amount?

2. First grade had a goal to sell at least 200 items. Did the grade meet its goal?

Second Grade:

1. How many more candles than rolls of gift wrap were sold?

2. For every 100 items sold, the second graders received a homework pass. How many homework passes have the second graders earned?

Third Grade:

1. What is the total number of items sold by the third graders?

2. How many more candles than rolls of gift wrap were sold?

Fourth Grade:

1. Fourth grade sold 65 candles. Of which item did they sell 30 more?

2. Of which two items did fourth grade sell the same amount?

- **All the grades have done quite well with their sales. Which grade, however, do you think is doing the best job? Explain your answer.**

Name ______________________________

HOME CONNECTION: PICTURE THIS

Dear Parent or Guardian:

Your child has been learning how to make and interpret pictographs. He or she has learned how to collect data, choose a symbol to represent the data, and then use the symbol in a pictograph. Your child will conduct a survey and complete pictographs to show the results.

Choose between 6 and 10 people to survey. They can be family members or friends (or both). Come up with two questions to ask each person, so that you can complete the two pictographs. Choose a symbol for each pictograph, and complete the key.

Days on Which People Watch the Most Television	
Sunday	
Monday	
Tuesday	
Wednesday	
Thursday	
Friday	
Saturday	

Key:

Favorite Kinds of Television Shows	

Key:

Name ______________________________

Stacked Up

CD-PLAYER COMPARISON

Brandy was comparing the prices of different types of CD players at the electronics store. She knew that some of the more expensive ones were a little bit better, but she didn't want to spend too much money. Below are the prices that she found.

Type of CD Player	Price (rounded to the nearest dollar)
Portable CD Player	$50.00
Mini-Disc Player	$140.00
Antishock CD Player	$75.00
ZRQ CD Player	$110.00
Portable CD Player Value Pack (with Headphones)	$60.00

Use the data from the table above to make a bar graph on page 11. After completing your bar graph, use it to help you answer questions 1–4.

1. What value did you use as your interval? Explain your reasoning.

2. What is the difference in price between a portable CD player and an antishock CD player?

3. What is the most expensive type of CD player?

4. Brandy found a pair of good headphones for $7.50. She wants to purchase a portable CD player with headphones. Should she purchase the value pack? Explain your reasoning.

Name ______________________________

COMPARISON DATA

Use the graph below to answer questions 1–4.

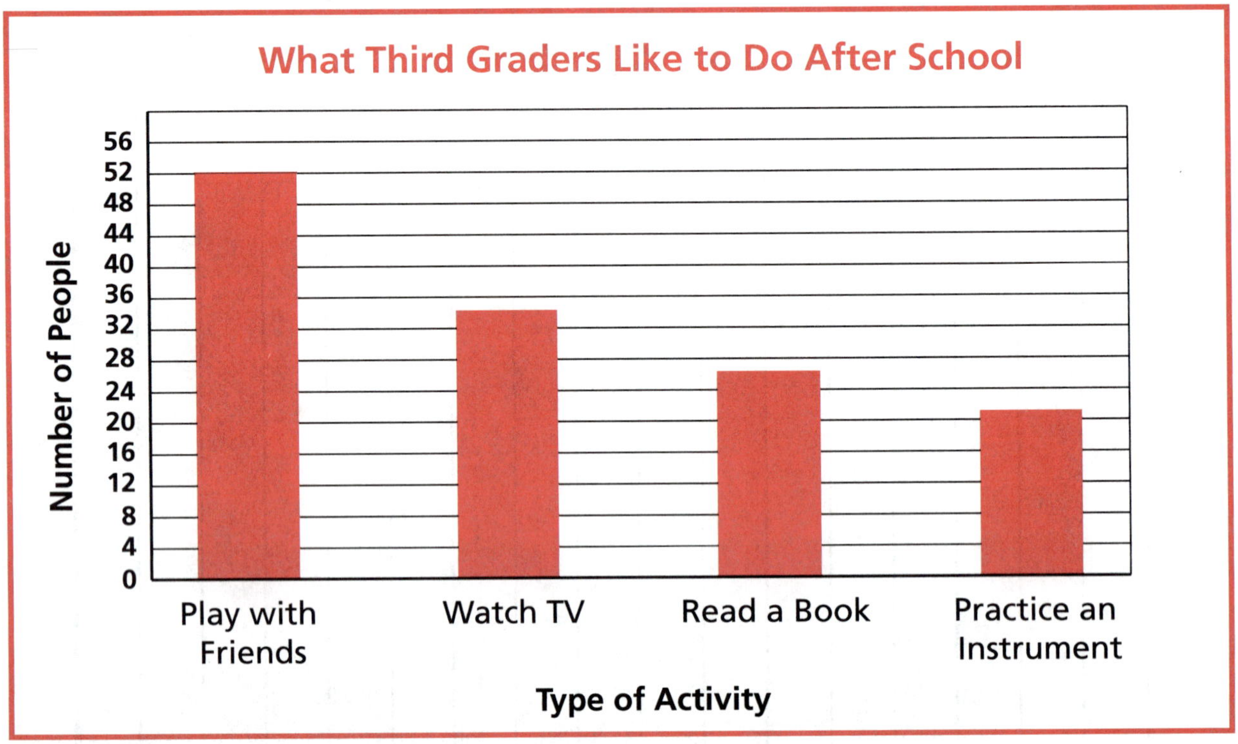

1. How many people said that they liked to watch TV after school?

2. Twice as many third graders liked to do this as to read a book. What is this activity?

3. What did the least number of third graders like to do after school?

4. What was the third graders' second favorite activity?

Name ______________________________

Sports League	Number of Teams in League
Major League Baseball (MLB)	30
National Hockey League (NHL)	30
Major League Soccer (MLS)	10
National Lacrosse League (NLL)	12
Women's National Basketball Association (WNBA)	15

Use the data from the table above to make a bar graph on the grid below.

DRIP-DROP EXPERIMENT

Purpose: To determine how many drops of water will fit onto the head of a penny, a nickel, a dime, and a quarter.

Prediction:

_________________ drops of water will fit onto the head of a penny.

_________________ drops of water will fit onto the head of a nickel.

_________________ drops of water will fit onto the head of a dime.

_________________ drops of water will fit onto the head of a quarter.

Procedure:

Materials (per group): eyedropper, penny, nickel, dime, quarter, cup of water, 4 paper towels

Step by Step:

1. Gather materials. (Data table must be labeled before conducting the experiment.)
2. Lay the paper towel on your desk and place one of your coins on the paper towel.
3. Fill the eyedropper with water.
4. Place drops of water onto the head of the coin, one at a time.
5. Count each drop.
6. Continue adding drops of water onto the head of the coin until the water spills off the coin and onto the paper towel.
7. Record the number of drops that the coin held on your data table. Be sure to record it in the correct space.
8. Use the paper towel to wipe off your desk and the coin.
9. Repeat steps 2–8 for the three remaining coins.
10. Clean up your work area and return the materials.
11. Record your observations.

Tell what you saw happen during the experiment. Did anything happen that you didn't expect?

1.

2.

Name ______________________________

Label the data table below so that you can use it to record the information collected during the experiment.

Use the data from your table to make a bar graph on the grid below. Remember to title your graph and to label the bars and the scale.

Tell whether your prediction was correct. Explain what you learned during the experiment. Do you have any questions about the experiment or the results?

HOME CONNECTION: KITCHEN COLLECTION

Dear Parent or Guardian:

Your child has been learning about bar graphs and how to use data to create a bar graph. Your child is going to practice the skills he or she has developed by gathering data from around your kitchen and using it as the basis for a bar graph. You can help her or him collect data about the contents of your kitchen pantry or cupboard. Your child will first need to decide upon categories to use. For example, he or she might count canned goods, paper products, cleaning products, boxed products, and snacks.

Use the table to record your data. Then use the grid to make a bar graph that shows your data. Be sure to label the scale and to title and label your bar graph. Add rows to your graph if needed.

Type of Kitchen Item	Number of Items

Name ______________________________

Double Stuff

CARD VALUES

Complete the chart by writing in the total number value of your cards by suit. Do the same with your partner's cards. Then make a double-bar graph to display the data.

	Clubs	Diamonds	Hearts	Spades
My Cards				
My Partner's Cards				

CLOUDY DAYS

Make a double-bar graph to show the data in the table.

Average Number of Cloudy Days by Season

	Spring	Summer	Fall	Winter
Tampa	26	34	29	32
Miami	30	34	28	25

Name ______________________________

Use your double-bar graph to answer the questions.

1. On the average, which season is the cloudiest?

2. During which season are Miami and Tampa most likely to have the same average number of cloudy days?

3. During which season is the average difference between cloudy days in Tampa and Miami the largest?

4. About how many cloudy days does Miami have each year?

5. About how many more cloudy days does Miami have than Tampa during the spring?

6. What is the average difference between the number of cloudy days during winter and the number of cloudy days during spring in Miami?

7. Which season is least cloudy in Tampa?

8. Approximately what fraction of the year is cloudy in Miami?

HOME CONNECTION: SURVEY AND GRAPH

Dear Parent or Guardian:

Your child has been learning how to make and interpret double-bar graphs. Now he or she is going to conduct a survey of family members and neighbors and display the collected data in a double-bar graph. To support your child's learning experience, review the completed bar graph. You should be able to tell easily what the bar graph is showing and to interpret the data on the graph.

Ask family members and friends what kind of fruit they like. Record responses to your survey question in the table. You can organize your data according to gender (males and females) or age (adults and children). Then make a double-bar graph to display your data.

Name ______________________________

Water Wise

SHOW THE DATA

Read each item. Choose the best way to show the information. Explain your answers.

Word Bank	
bar graph	tally table
data table	line graph

1. Lucy wants to record the number of times she turns on a water faucet in her house in one day.

2. Sam is collecting data about the average rainfall per year in different countries. So far, he has found data for three of the ten countries he wants to research.

3. Javier collects data about the average monthly rainfall in Brazil during one year. He wants to make it easy to see when the wettest time of the year occurs.

4. Janelle wants to keep track of the amount of water her family uses at dinner each day for a week.

5. Francisco has researched the amount of water used in one day in five different schools. He wants to show his data so that he can easily see how the amounts compare.

KINDS OF GRAPHS AND WHAT THEY SHOW

Use the graph to answer questions 1–4.

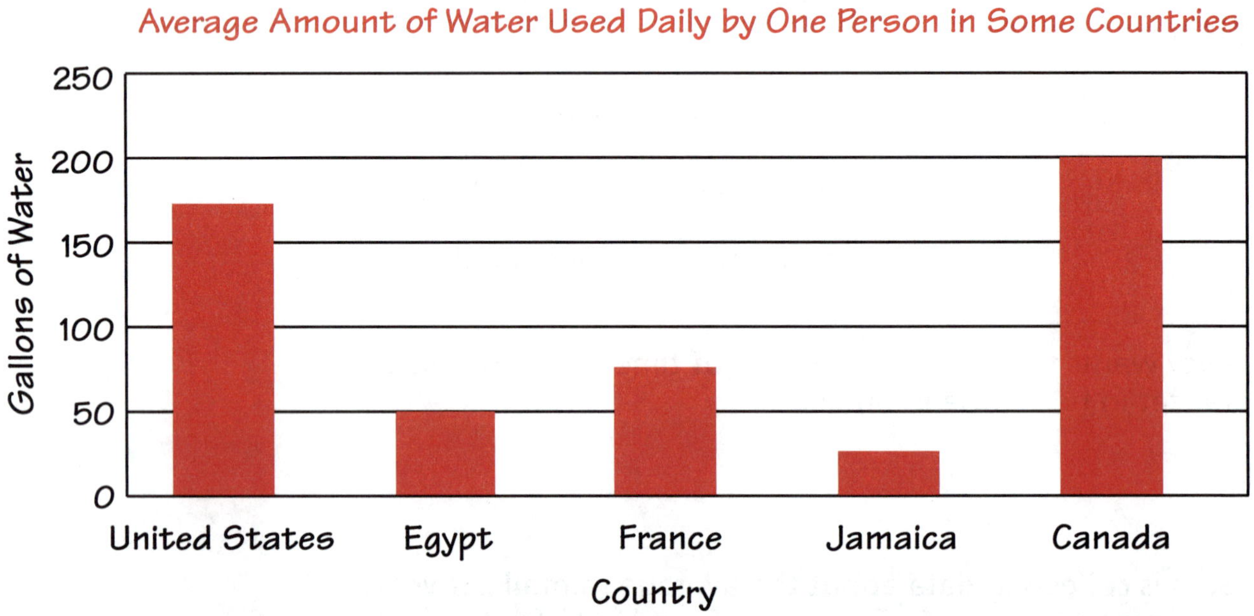

1. What does the scale show? What is the interval?

2. In which country does one person use the least amount of water per day?

3. About how many gallons of water does a person use each day in France?

4. About how many more gallons of water does a person use in Canada than a person in the United States? How did you find the answer?

Name ______________________________

Use the graph to solve problems 5–8.

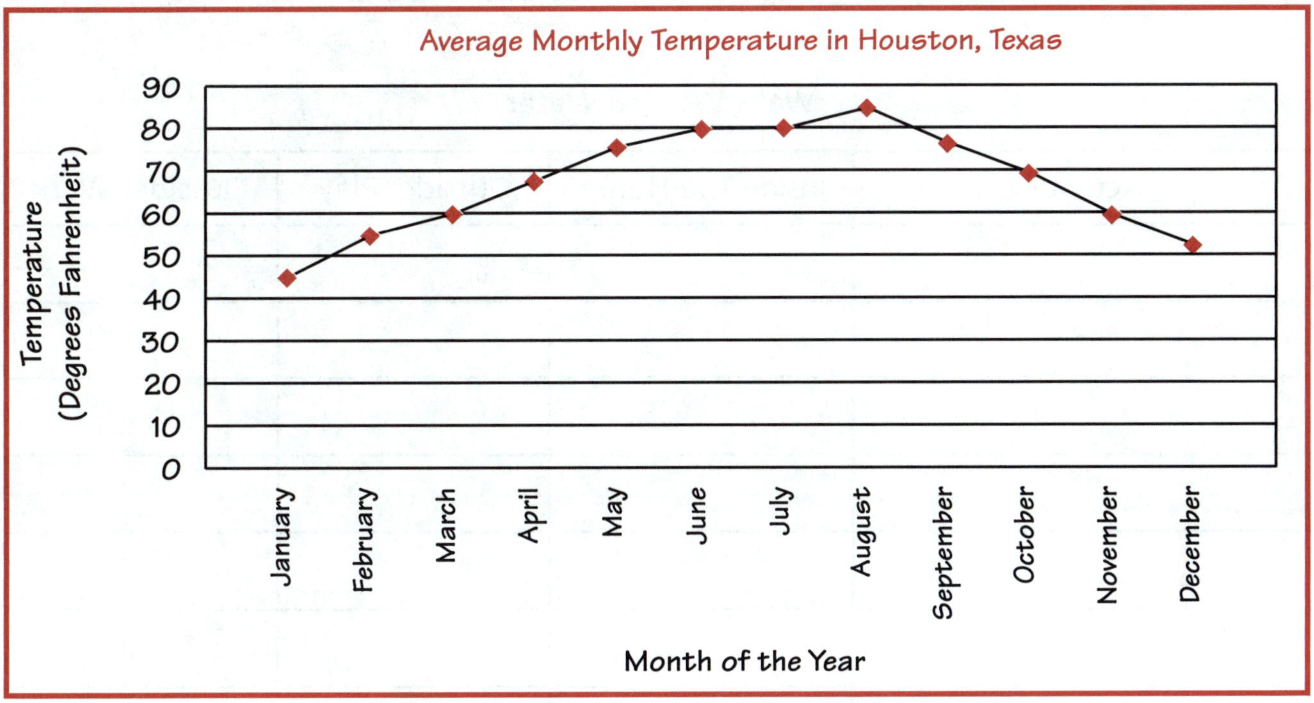

5. If you plan to take a trip to Houston in June, about how high should you expect the temperature to be?

6. What is the approximate difference between the temperature of the warmest month and the temperature of the coolest month? How did you find the answer?

7. Describe what happens to Houston's average temperature from August to November.

8. In Atlanta, Georgia, the average temperature in January is about 40 degrees. Compare the January temperature of Atlanta to the January temperature of Houston.

WATER SAVERS

Record information from your group's water cards in this table.

Ways We Use Water

Activity	Inside the Home	Outside: Play	Outside: Work
Totals:			

Name ____

Use the totals from your Water Savers data table to create a graph. Title and label your graph.

____

Discuss your Water Savers data table and Water Savers graph with the other members of your group. Then answer the questions.

1. What was different about the white water cards and the gray water cards?

2. What was the total amount of water used by the groups with the white water cards?

3. What was the total amount of water used by the groups with the gray water cards?

Use the gray and white water cards to make a list of water-saving techniques. Calculate the amount of water that can be saved by using them. An example is done for you.

Water-Saving Technique	Water Use with Technique	Water Use Without Technique	Gallons of Water Saved
Watering lawn in the evening instead of during the day	120	180	60

Name ______________________________

HOME CONNECTION: FAVORITE DRINKS

Dear Parent or Guardian:

Your child has been learning how to collect data and then show the data on a bar graph or line graph. To practice his or her skills at data collection and analysis, your child will be conducting a survey among family members and neighbors to find out what people prefer to drink. The choices your child will be using are water, milk, juice, soda, and other beverage. Your child will then use the collected data to make a vertical bar graph.

You can help your child by suggesting at least 10 relatives or neighbors your child might interview. He or she can keep track of the data in the table on the reverse side of this page. Once the data has been collected, your child should be able to show it on a bar graph, using the form provided. You should be able to understand clearly what the bar graph shows.

Survey family members and friends to find out what they prefer to drink. Use the choices in the tally table. Record people's choices in the tally table.

Then use the data you collect to make a vertical bar graph. Be sure to title your graph and to write labels and the scale.

What My Family and Neighbors Like to Drink

Kind of Drink	Tallies
Water	
Milk	
Juice	
Soda	
Other Beverages	

Name ______________________________

Taking a Closer Look

¡COLOR SQUARE FIESTA!

Using a crayon, color in the squares beneath each color. Then, cut out each square to help you arrange your data and answer the questions below.

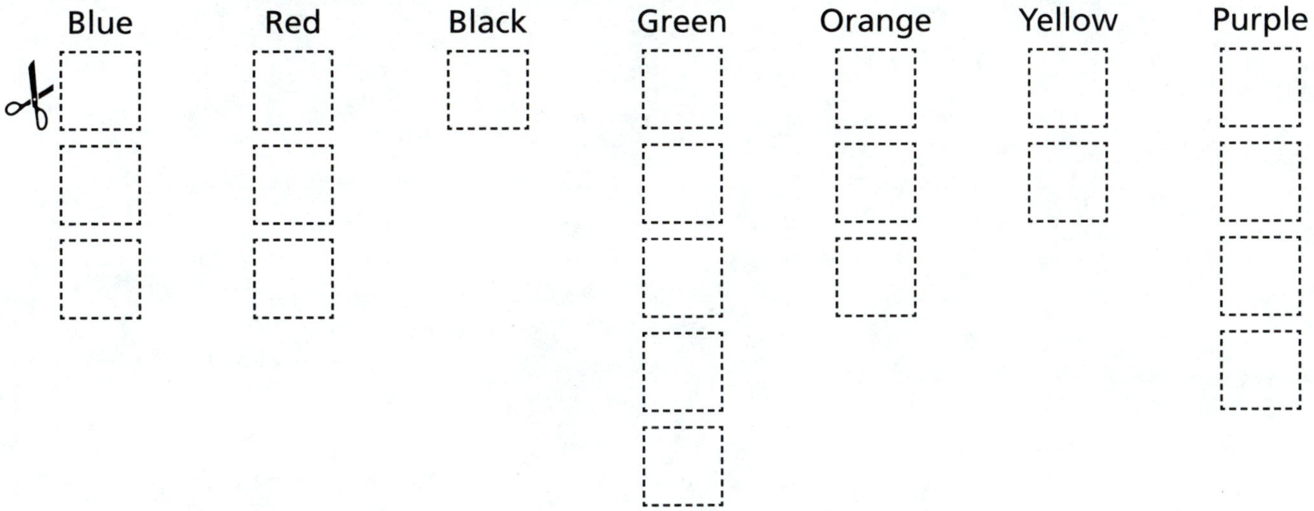

1. What is the mean (average) number of squares per color? (This can be found by moving squares until each column has the same number of squares.)

   ____

2. Look at the blue, orange, and red pieces.

   How many pieces of each are there? ______________

   This is the __ __ D __ because there are more 3s than any other number.

3. Order the colors from least to greatest.

   What color is in the middle? ______________

   How many pieces of this color are there? ______________

   This is the __ E __ __ __ N because it is the middle number in a set of data.

4. Which color has the least number of pieces? ______________

   Which color has the greatest number of pieces? ______________

   What is the difference between the two colors? ______________

   This is the __ A __ __ __ because it is the difference between the greatest and the least values.

Name ______________________________

LOOKING FOR THE CENTER AND MORE

Write the five numbers from each station on the lines below. Then, using cubes, find the mean, median, mode, and range for each set of numbers.

Station 1

Set of Numbers: { _____, _____, _____, _____, _____ }

Mean = _____ **Median =** _____ **Mode =** _____ **Range =** _____

Station 2

Set of Numbers: { _____, _____, _____, _____, _____ }

Mean = _____ **Median =** _____ **Mode =** _____ **Range =** _____

Station 3

Set of Numbers: { _____, _____, _____, _____, _____ }

Mean = _____ **Median =** _____ **Mode =** _____ **Range =** _____

Station 4

Set of Numbers: { _____, _____, _____, _____, _____ }

Mean = _____ **Median =** _____ **Mode =** _____ **Range =** _____

Station 5

Set of Numbers: { _____, _____, _____, _____, _____ }

Mean = _____ **Median =** _____ **Mode =** _____ **Range =** _____

HOME CONNECTION: TAKING A SURVEY

Dear Parent or Guardian:

Your child has been learning about finding the range, mean, median, and mode of a set of data. Now your child is going to choose a survey question, conduct a survey of 10 people, record the gathered data (survey responses), and find the range, mean, median, and mode of the gathered data.

Write your survey question. Ask 10 people your question. Record the responses in a tally chart or a table. Find the range, mean, median, and mode of your set of data.

Survey Question:

Responses:

Range:

Mean:

Median:

Mode:

TOPIC 2

Whole Numbers and Decimals I

Name ______________________________

And the Winning Number Is . . .

SACKS OF PLENTY

Use estimation to find the sack with the greatest value and the sack with the least value. Special recognition will go to the team with the most accurate estimate of the value of each sack.

Select a member of your team to estimate the value of the first sack. After that, rotate the position so that everyone has a chance to practice estimating. Record your results in the table.

Sack	1	2	3	4	5	6	7	8	9
Estimated Value									

1. Which sack do you think has the greatest value?

2. Which sack do you think has the least value?

With your team, calculate the actual value of each sack. Find the difference between each estimate and each actual value. Record your results in the table.

Sack	1	2	3	4	5	6	7	8	9
Actual Value									
Difference									

3. What were your team's five most accurate estimates?

4. If you were to play Sacks of Plenty again, would you change your estimation strategy? Explain.

GEOLOGY TODAY

In the game show Geology Today, winners pick their own prizes. Today, the prizes are necklaces made with four kinds of stones. Use the chart to solve the problem.

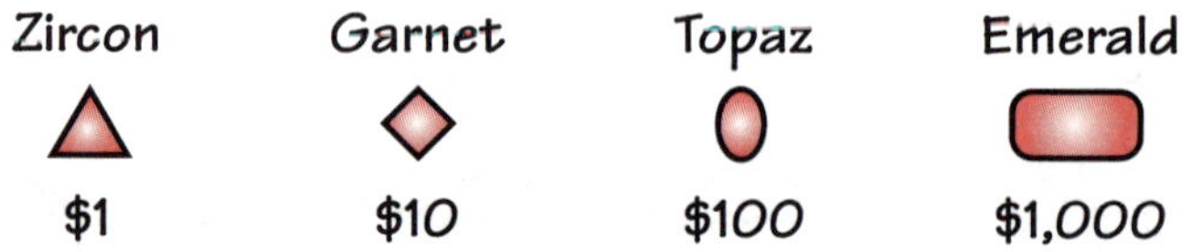

1. After winning a round, Ms. Chan gets to choose one of two necklaces. If she wants the most valuable necklace, which should she choose?

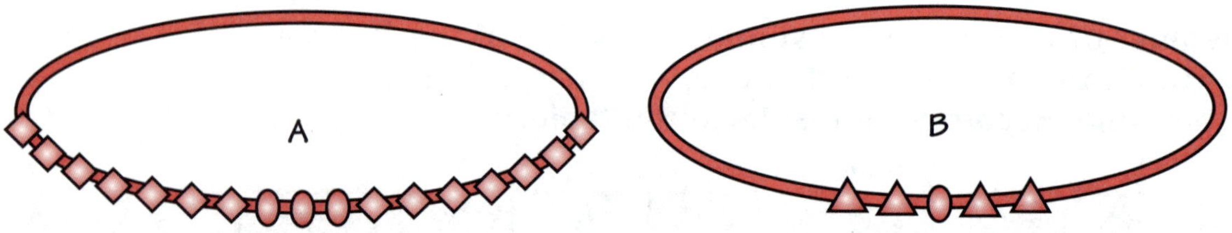

2. Wilfred wins a round, and can choose one of two necklaces. If he wants the most valuable necklace, which should he pick?

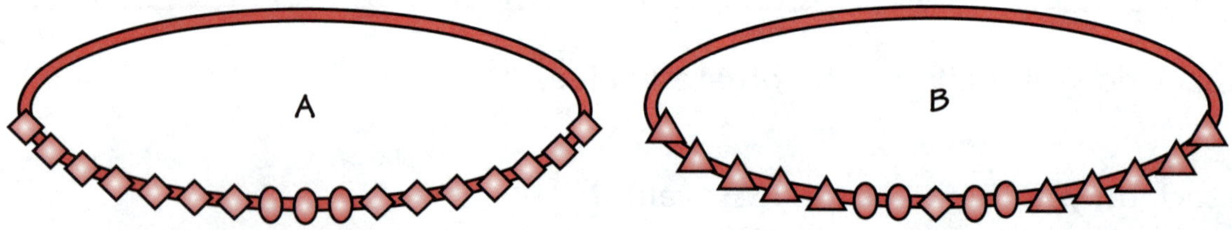

3. Anne takes the lead by correctly describing the eruption of volcanoes. If she wants the most valuable necklace, which should she choose?

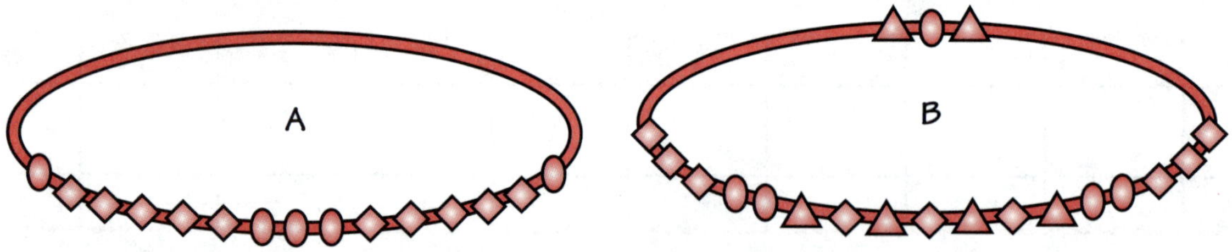

4. Ms. Chan wins the final round by identifying the Colorado River. If she wants the most valuable necklace, which should she pick?

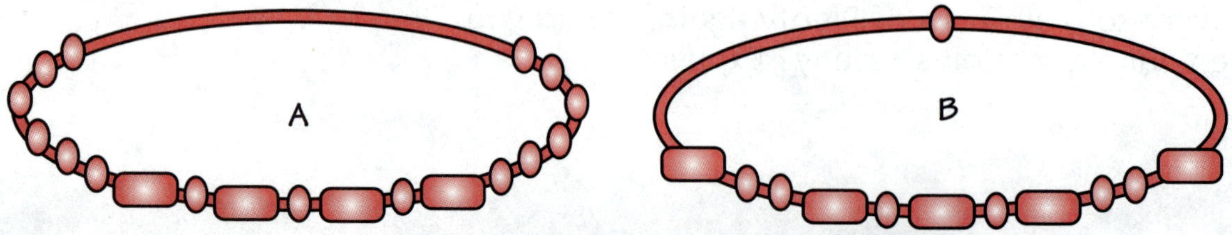

Name ______________________________

5. Draw necklace B so that it has the same value as necklace A. Draw a different set of stones for necklace B.

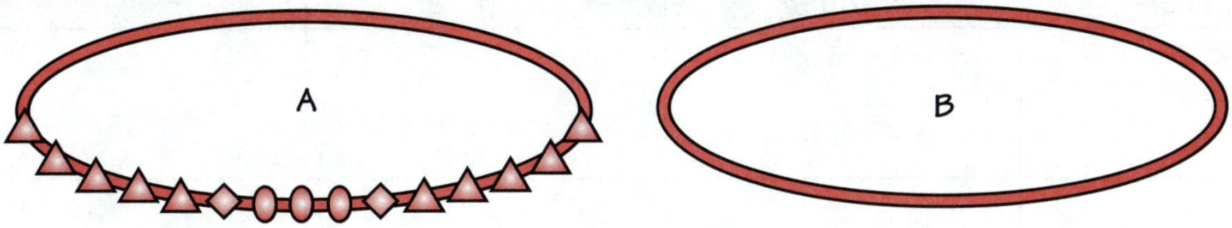

6. Draw **more** stones for necklace B. Make necklace B have the same value as necklace A.

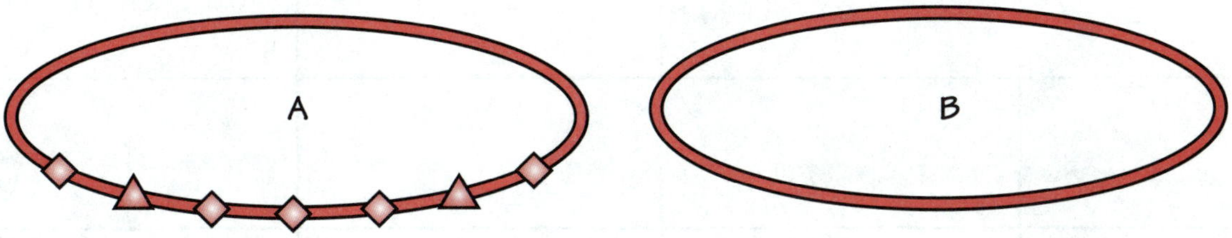

7. Draw **fewer** stones for necklace B. Make necklace B have the same value as necklace A.

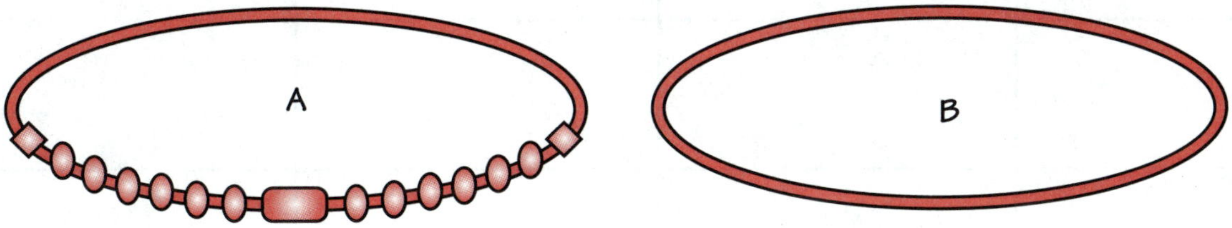

8. Draw two different necklaces that each have a value of $275.

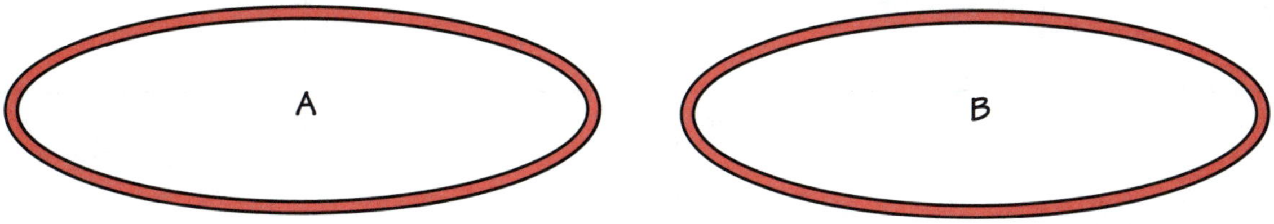

9. Draw two different necklaces that each have a value of $1,000.

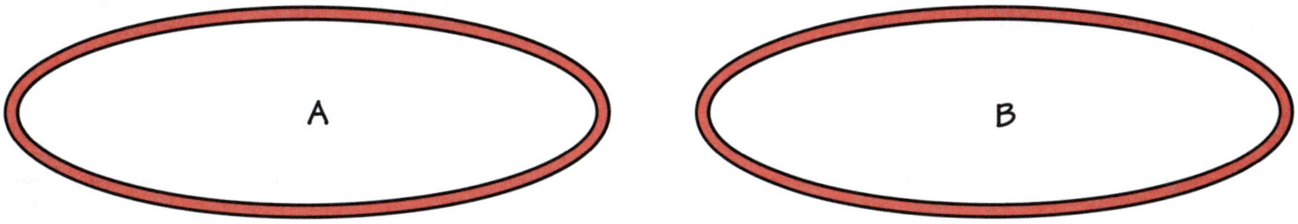

FOUR IN A ROW WORKSHEET

Four Digits Called	Greatest Number	Least Number	My Points

Name ______________________________

HOME CONNECTION: FOUR IN A ROW

Dear Parent or Guardian:

Your child has been learning the place values of numbers to ten thousands. In class, your child has played a game called Four in a Row. You, your child, and other family members can play the same game. Use the game cards below. Have one person call out digits randomly. Each player covers the digits on his or her card that have been called. Any four digits in a horizontal, vertical, or diagonal "row" makes four in a row. A player with four in a row has a given period (say 20 seconds) to name the greatest number and the least number that can be made with those four digits. If the player does so correctly, he or she gets a point. (For example, with the digits 4, 9, 2, and 5, the greatest number possible is 9,542; while the least number possible is 2,459.)

Cut out the game cards and play Four in a Row with members of your family.

2	0	8	5	5	2	1	9	2	5	9	6
7	5	9	3	6	9	0	7	7	0	8	1
1	7	4	0	4	8	3	2	8	1	3	2
4	6	8	6	5	7	4	8	5	0	4	7
9	4	8	3	1	5	3	2	6	5	0	1
2	5	7	1	9	6	0	7	3	7	2	5
6	0	8	9	3	8	5	4	2	8	4	1
1	2	5	6	4	7	2	1	0	6	3	9

Name ____________________

Balancing Acts

THE POINT OF BALANCE

Use base-ten manipulatives and a balance to find the missing number.

1. 19 + _______ = 8 + 25
2. 6 + 11 = 9 + _______
3. _______ + 7 = 10 + 9
4. 30 + 6 = _______ + 16
5. 60 + 50 = _______ + 80
6. _______ + 10 = 38 + 17
7. 70 + 90 = 100 + _______
8. 203 + _______ = 180 + 40
9. 24 + 46 = _______ + 35
10. _______ + 30 = 65 + 75

Use base-ten manipulatives and a balance to solve the inequality. Write < or >.

11. 8 + 12 _______ 9 + 9
12. 15 + 7 _______ 4 + 20
13. 33 + 20 _______ 24 + 30
14. 11 + 58 _______ 25 + 41
15. 50 + 90 _______ 90 + 45
16. 230 + 16 _______ 45 + 205
17. 62 + 8 _______ 35 + 31
18. 15 + 80 _______ 7 + 79
19. 51 + 130 _______ 48 + 140
20. 14 + 19 _______ 15 + 20

MASSIVE NUMBERS

Draw base-ten manipulatives to make the sides balance. Then complete the equation.

1.

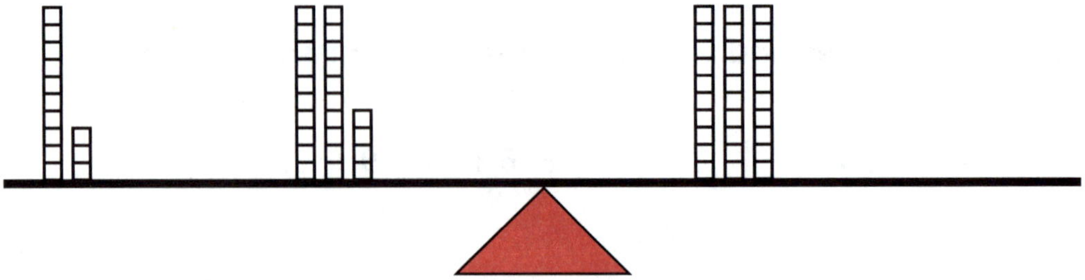

13 + 24 = 30 + ______

2.

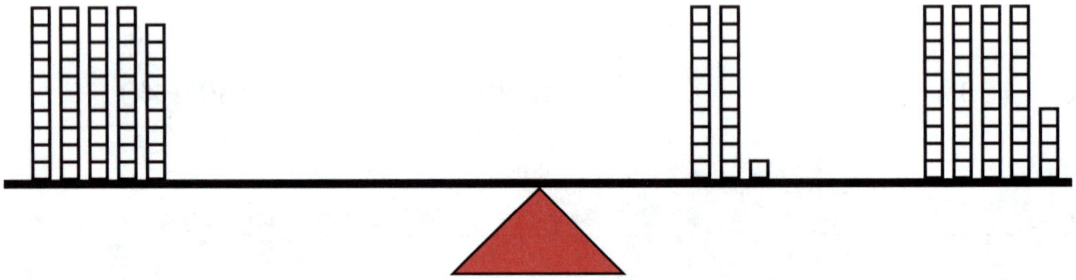

49 + ______ = 21 + 44

3.

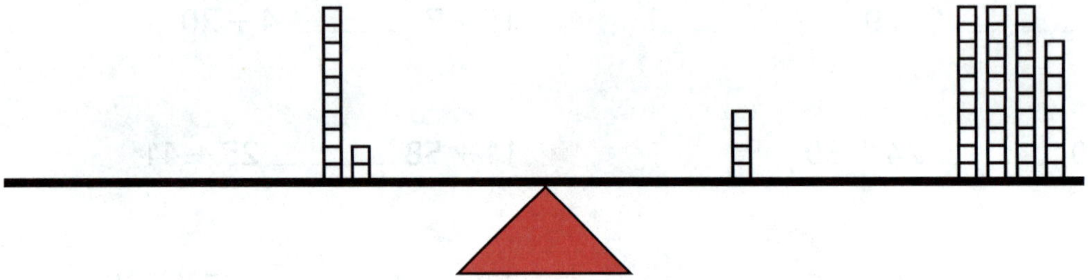

______ + 12 = 4 + ______

4.

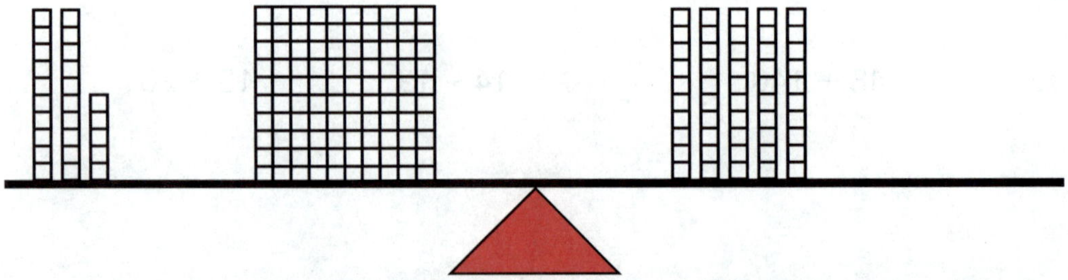

______ + 100 = 50 + ______

Name ______________________________

Write the missing number(s). Ring the side of the balance that will fall when the mathematician removes her finger. Complete the inequality by writing < or >.

5.

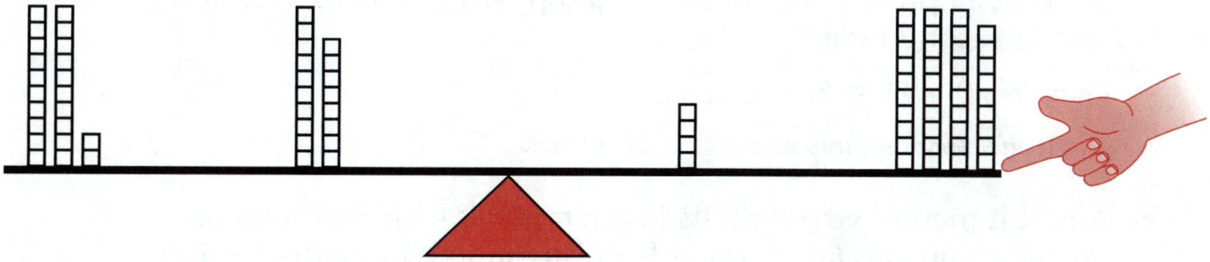

22 + 18 ____ 4 + ____

6.

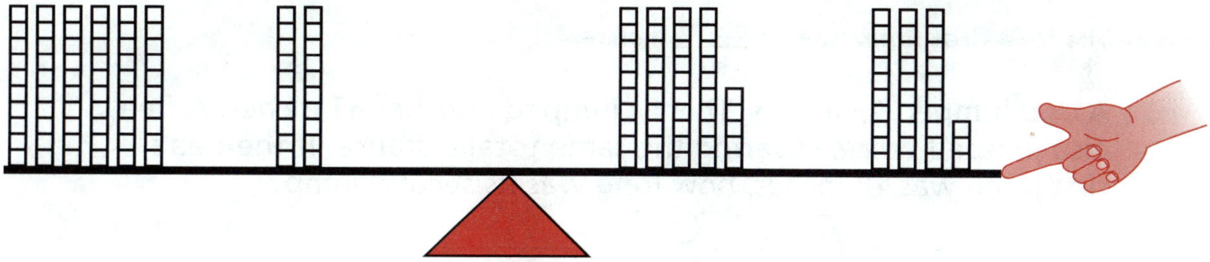

60 + ____ ____ 45 + ____

7.

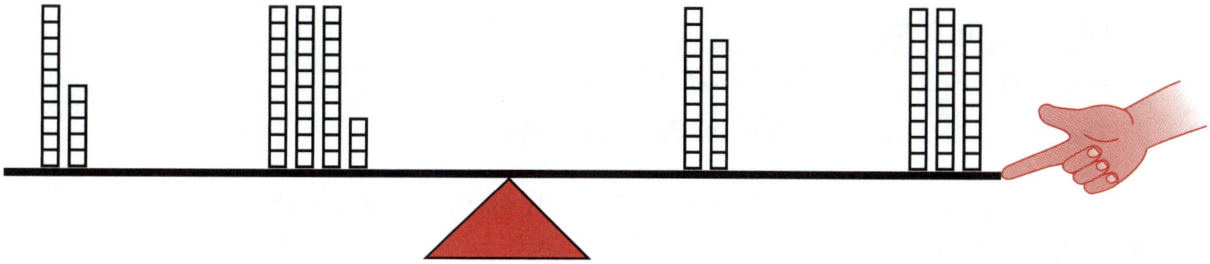

____ + ____ ____ 18 + 29

8.

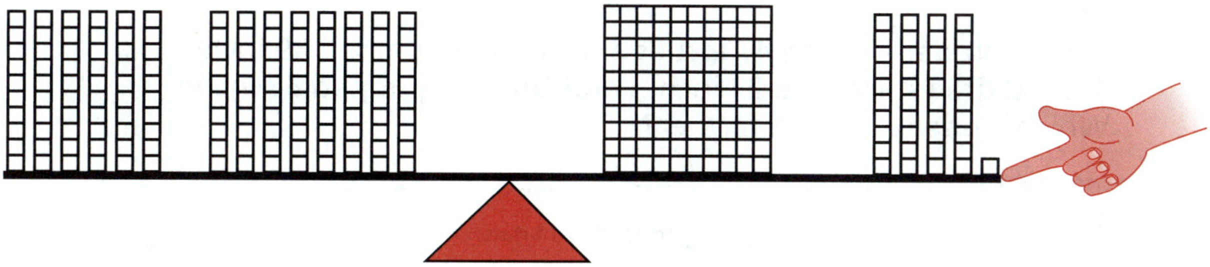

____ + 80 ____ 100 + ____

JUMPING PATTERNS

Write an equation or inequality to show the problem. Then solve it.

1. A grasshopper jumped 9 inches. Then it jumped 25 inches. A frog also jumped twice. It jumped the same total number of inches as the grasshopper. If the frog's first jump was 21 inches, how long was its second jump?

   Equation: 9 + 25 = 21 + ______

   The frog's second jump was ______ inches.

2. A rabbit made two jumps. Its first jump was 43 inches, and its second jump was 66 inches. A fox also made two jumps, for the same total distance. If the fox's second jump was 59 inches, how long was its first jump?

   Equation: ______ + 66 = ______ + ______

   The fox's first jump was ______ inches.

3. A dog jumped 15 inches. Then it jumped another 37 inches. A flea also jumped twice, covering the same total distance. If the flea's first jump was 28 inches, how long was its second jump?

   Equation: ______________ ◯ ______________

   The flea's second jump was ______ inches.

4. A deer jumped 66 inches and then it jumped 70 inches. A cougar jumped 90 inches and then it jumped 51 inches. Which animal jumped farther?

   Inequality: ______ + 70 ◯ 90 + 51

   The ______________ jumped farther.

5. A kangaroo jumped 212 inches. Then it jumped 185 inches. A dingo jumped 96 inches. Then it jumped 123 inches. Which animal jumped farther?

   Inequality: 212 + ______ ◯ ______ + 123

   The ______________ jumped farther.

6. A fifth grader jumped 47 inches and then he jumped 39 inches. A third grader jumped 22 inches and then he jumped 68 inches. Which student jumped farther?

   Inequality: ______________ ◯ ______________

   The ______________ jumped farther.

Name ____

HOME CONNECTION: WRITE YOUR OWN PROBLEMS

Dear Parent or Guardian:

Your child has been learning about equations and inequalities. In an equation, such as $25 + 10 = 30 + 5$, both sides "balance" at the equal sign. In an inequality, such as $22 + 4 > 15 + 8$, one side is greater than the other. For this assignment, your child will find weights of food items in your kitchen (or refrigerator) and use these weights to write his or her own equation and inequality.

Find items in your kitchen or refrigerator that show the items' weights. For example, a loaf of bread might weigh 1 lb, a bag of rice might weigh 5 lb, and a can of beans might weigh 2 lb. Draw some of the items on each side of the balance so that the sides balance. Label the weight of each item. Then write an equation for your drawing.

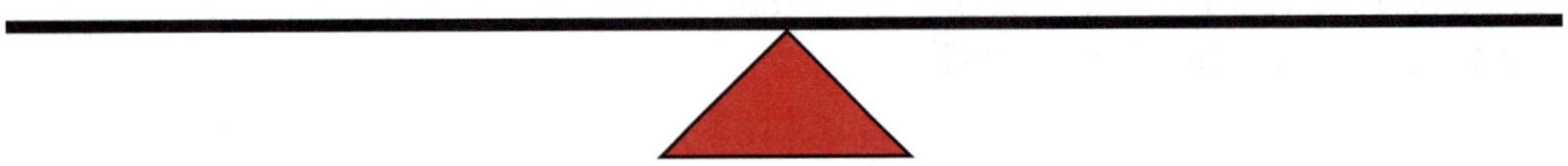

Equation: ______________________________

Draw some of the items on each side of the balance so that the sides don't balance. Label the weight of each item. Then write an inequality for your drawing.

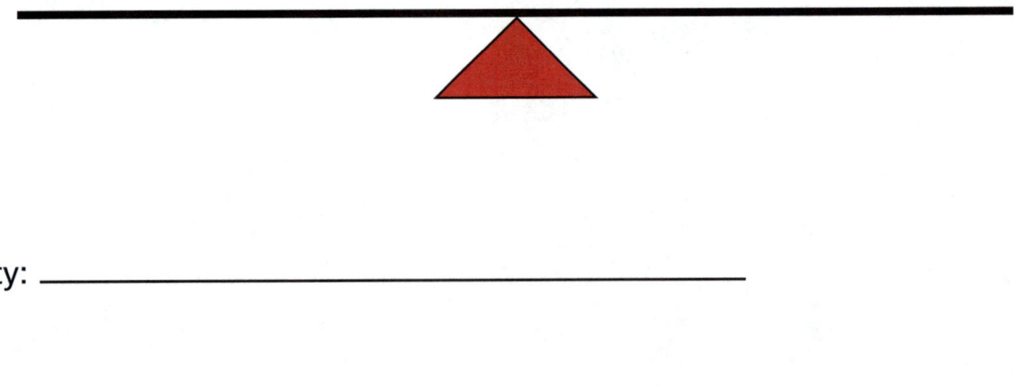

Inequality: ______________________________

Name ______________________________

A Ballpark Figure

SPIN AND ROUND!

Place a paper clip over the center point of the circle. Place the tip of your pencil through the paper clip on the center point of the circle. Flick the paper clip to conduct each spin.

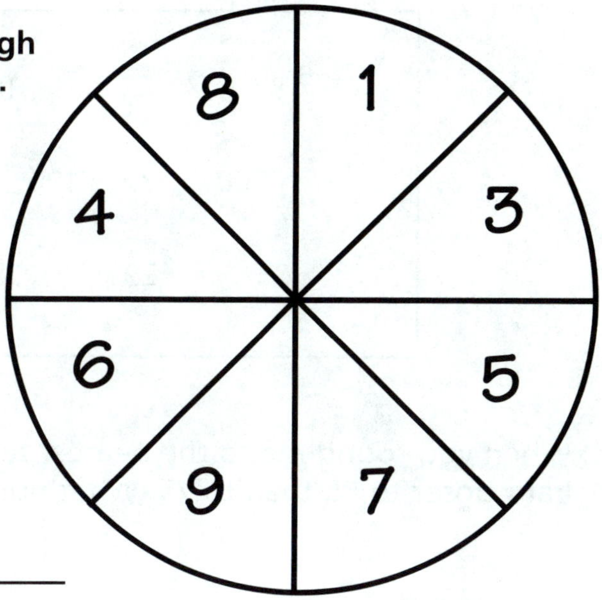

Record each spun number in order on the lines provided. Then round the number to the nearest ten.

Example: Spin 1: 8
Spin 2: 4

8 **4** → **8** **0**

1.

______ (Spin 1) ______ (Spin 2) → ______ ______

2.

______ (Spin 1) ______ (Spin 2) → ______ ______

3.

______ (Spin 1) ______ (Spin 2) → ______ ______

Record 3 spins and round to the nearest hundred.

4.

______ (Spin 1) ______ (Spin 2) ______ (Spin 3) → ______ ______ ______

5.

______ (Spin 1) ______ (Spin 2) ______ (Spin 3) → ______ ______ ______

6.

______ (Spin 1) ______ (Spin 2) ______ (Spin 3) → ______ ______ ______

7.

______ (Spin 1) ______ (Spin 2) ______ (Spin 3) → ______ ______ ______

ROUNDING RIDDLES

Read each riddle. Then write a number from the box that answers the riddle. Cross out each number as you use it. You will not use all the numbers in the box.

87	65	14	170	64		
260	7	190	210	310	33	
35	29	650	550	83		

1. When you round me to the nearest ten, the number is 80. I am closer to 85 than to 75. What number am I?

2. When you round me to the nearest ten, the number is 70. I am somewhere between 61 and 69. What number am I?

3. When you round me to the nearest hundred, the number is 200. I am closer to 250 than to 150. What number am I?

4. If you round me to the nearest hundred, the number is 300. When you round me, you would be rounding up. What number am I?

5. I am not quite halfway between 30 and 40. If you round me to the nearest ten, the number is 30. What number am I?

6. I am halfway between 600 and another hundred. If you round me up to the nearest hundred, the number is not 600. What number am I?

Name ______________________________

HOME CONNECTION: AGES UP OR DOWN

Dear Parent or Guardian:

Your child has been learning how to round whole numbers to the nearest ten and hundred. He or she has learned how to round down to the nearest ten if the digit in the ones place is under 5 and to round up if the digit in the ones place is 5 or more. This activity is designed to give your child practice using his or her skill at rounding. On the reverse side of this page, your child will record the ages of family members and/or relatives and neighbors and then round the ages to the nearest ten. If your child wants to, he or she may make drawings of the people.

You can reinforce your child's understanding of rounding by having him or her explain to you how each person's age was rounded.

Find the ages of four or five people you know. Record each person's age and then write what the number would be if the age were rounded to the nearest ten. Hint: Do not use ages that are multiples of 10. In the space beside each rounded number, you can draw a picture of the person and tell who the person is.

	Person's Exact Age	Person's Age Rounded to the Nearest Ten	Drawing of Person
1.			
2.			
3.			
4.			
5.			

Name ______________________________

Alternative Algorithms

MORE WAYS TO ADD

Use the Compensation Algorithm for addition to solve items 1–4. The first one has been done for you.

1.
```
  486   (+14)    500
+ 222   (-14)  + 208
                 708
```

2.
```
  821
+ 698
```

3.
```
  1,289
+   951
```

4.
```
  727
+ 447
```

Use the Partial-Sums Algorithm to solve items 5–8.

5.
```
                          3,897
                         +2,024
Add the thousands.        5,000
Add the hundreds.           800
Add the tens.               110
Add the ones.                11
                          5,921
```

6.
```
  8,052
 +1,947
```

7.
```
  886
+ 727
```

8.
```
  73,951
 +37,865
```

DIFFERENT WAYS TO SUBTRACT

Use the Compensation Algorithm for subtraction to solve the problems. Show your work. The first one has been done for you.

1.

1,881	+19	1,900
−1,681	+19	−1,700
		200

2.

$$\begin{array}{r} 1{,}941 \\ -1{,}591 \\ \hline \end{array}$$

3.

$$\begin{array}{r} 7{,}477 \\ -5{,}427 \\ \hline \end{array}$$

4.

$$\begin{array}{r} 536 \\ -\ 454 \\ \hline \end{array}$$

5.

$$\begin{array}{r} 24{,}701 \\ -20{,}056 \\ \hline \end{array}$$

6.

$$\begin{array}{r} 49{,}600 \\ -38{,}025 \\ \hline \end{array}$$

Name ____

DIFFERENT WAYS TO THE SAME SOLUTION

Solve each problem two different ways. Use what you know about finding partial sums and using compensation for addition and subtraction. After you solve each problem two different ways, circle the way that was easiest for you.

1. $\begin{array}{r} 467 \\ +\ 825 \\ \hline \end{array}$

2. $\begin{array}{r} 356 \\ -\ 288 \\ \hline \end{array}$

3. $\begin{array}{r} 2{,}321 \\ -2{,}145 \\ \hline \end{array}$

4. $\begin{array}{r} 978 \\ +\ 622 \\ \hline \end{array}$

5. $\begin{array}{r} 23{,}890 \\ -4{,}732 \\ \hline \end{array}$

6. $\begin{array}{r} 764 \\ +\ 278 \\ \hline \end{array}$

7. $\begin{array}{r} 607 \\ +\ 393 \\ \hline \end{array}$

8. $\begin{array}{r} 4{,}712 \\ -2{,}288 \\ \hline \end{array}$

9. $\begin{array}{r} 2{,}948 \\ +1{,}172 \\ \hline \end{array}$

10. $\begin{array}{r} 29{,}742 \\ -17{,}398 \\ \hline \end{array}$

Name ______________________________

HOME CONNECTION: EASY NUMBERS

Dear Parent or Guardian:

Your child has been learning about different procedures that can make solving addition and subtraction problems easier. In mathematics, such step-by-step procedures are called *algorithms*. One algorithm your child has learned is the Compensation Algorithm. This algorithm can make adding two numbers or subtracting one number from another easier. To reinforce understanding of the Compensation Algorithm, have your child explain the steps of the algorithm to you as he or she works through the addition and subtraction problems on the reverse side of this page. One addition problem and one subtraction problem have been done for your child to refresh his or her memory of the algorithm. These are followed by several problems that your child can solve on his or her own.

Explain to a family member the steps of the Compensation Algorithm used to solve the first two problems. Then use the Compensation Algorithm to solve the remaining addition and subtraction problems.

The Compensation Algorithm for addition

$$\begin{array}{r} 578 \\ +\ 322 \\ \hline \end{array} \quad \begin{array}{r} +22 \\ -22 \end{array} \quad \begin{array}{c} = \\ = \end{array} \quad \begin{array}{r} 600 \\ +\ 300 \\ \hline 900 \end{array}$$

The Compensation Algorithm for subtraction

$$\begin{array}{r} 462 \\ -\ 256 \\ \hline \end{array} \quad \begin{array}{r} -6 \\ -6 \end{array} \quad \begin{array}{c} = \\ = \end{array} \quad \begin{array}{r} 456 \\ -\ 250 \\ \hline 206 \end{array} \quad \begin{array}{r} -50 \\ -50 \end{array} \quad \begin{array}{c} = \\ = \end{array} \quad \begin{array}{r} 406 \\ -\ 200 \\ \hline 206 \end{array}$$

1. $\begin{array}{r} 396 \\ +\ 294 \\ \hline \end{array}$

2. $\begin{array}{r} 617 \\ -\ 327 \\ \hline \end{array}$

3. $\begin{array}{r} 2{,}279 \\ -\ 861 \\ \hline \end{array}$

4. $\begin{array}{r} 2{,}881 \\ -1{,}691 \\ \hline \end{array}$

Name ____

Wishful Thinking

DARRYL'S DOLLARS AND DOUGHNUTS

Solve 3 problems using mental math, 3 problems with a calculator, and 4 problems with pencil and paper. Write M for mental math, C for calculator, and P for pencil and paper.

1. Darryl sells a dozen doughnuts for $8. If you bought 12 doughnuts and gave him $20, how much change should you get?

2. Each doughnut costs 75¢. How much would 5 doughnuts cost?

3. Mrs. Cantor paid $37.25 for doughnuts and $28.60 for iced tea for the class picnic. How much did she pay in all?

4. Valerie bought 7 doughnuts for $5.25. She paid Darryl with a $10 bill. How much change did she get?

5. Melissa has $10 in her pocket. If two dozen doughnuts cost $16.00, how much more money does she need to buy them?

6. Darryl charges \$4.45 for a sandwich and 75¢ for a doughnut. How much more does a sandwich cost than a doughnut?

7. Darryl charges \$40 for 5 dozen doughnuts. Devon's Delicacies charges \$50 for 5 dozen doughnuts. How much less do 5 dozen doughnuts cost at Darryl's than at Devon's?

8. Kirk buys doughnuts for his friends at work each day. Last week, he paid \$1.50, \$8, \$7.50, \$3.00, \$6.75, \$8, and \$5.25 for doughnuts. How much did he pay for doughnuts in all last week?

9. Jenny paid \$9.50 for 14 doughnuts. Jack bought 9 doughnuts for \$6.75. How much more did Jenny pay than Jack did?

10. Shannon bought 6 doughnuts for \$4.50. She also paid \$3.75 for fruit juices. How much did she pay in all?

Name ______________________________

DINA'S DELI DELIGHTS

Ham and Cheese Sandwich	$3.00
Turkey Sandwich	$2.25
Chicken Sandwich	$2.00
Can of Juice	$0.65
Carton of Milk	$0.35
Apple	$0.25
Muffin	$0.40

Use the menu above to solve problems 1-5.

1. You have $3 to spend at Dina's Deli Delights. You buy a turkey sandwich and an apple. How much money do you have left?

2. How much would it cost to buy every item on the menu?

3. How much would it cost to buy 2 ham and cheese sandwiches and 2 chicken sanwiches?

4. You give Dina two dollars and four dimes. You get a nickel back. Which 2 items did you buy?

5. What is the difference in price between the least and most expensive items?

6. Lauren earned $80 baby-sitting last week. Sam earned $65 baby-sitting last week. How much less money did Sam earn than Lauren?

7. Steve bought five packs of baseball cards. Each pack costs $1.89. If he paid with a $10 bill, how much change should he receive?

8. Manuel's father gave him $20.00 for his birthday. Manuel used the money to buy a CD that cost $14.67. How much money does Manuel have left?

9. Ann bought 3 sweaters that cost $25.45, $32.60, and $30.49. If she gave the clerk $100, how much change did she get?

10. Lynne paid $9.25 to see a movie at the movie theater. The next day she rented a video for $4.75. How much did she pay in all for the movie and the video?

Name ____

HOME CONNECTION: COUNTING COUPONS

Dear Parent or Guardian:

Your child has been learning about adding and subtracting amounts of money. He or she has also been learning how to choose an appropriate method for solving a problem—such as using mental math or using a calculator.

Please help your child choose and cut out 5 coupons from the newspaper. Your child should tape or glue the coupons on this page, and then use them to solve the problems on the next page.

Solve the problem. For problems 1–3, tell whether you used mental math, a calculator, or pencil and paper to find the solution.

1. What is the total value of all your coupons?

2. If you could use all your coupons 2 times each, how much money would you save?

3. What is the difference in value between the coupon with the greatest value and the coupon with the least value?

4. What is the total value of all your coupons rounded to the nearest dollar?

5. Would you trade a $10 bill for all your coupons? Explain your answer.

6. Check the expiration dates of your coupons. What is the earliest expiration date?

Name ______________________________

Castaways with Cash

AT THE FRONT

Use front-end estimation to solve the problems. Show your work. Explain whether or not you think front-end estimation was a good form of estimation to use for each situation.

1. Use front-end estimation to estimate the sum of 372, 954, and 129.

2. If you buy two items that cost $3.21 each, will $5.00 be enough to buy both items? Explain your thinking.

3. Tickets to a history museum cost $2.50 for adults and $1.50 for students. Is $4.00 enough to buy tickets for 2 adults and 1 student? Explain your thinking.

4. Clark bought 96 ft of rope. He used 41 ft of rope to make Lois's clothesline. About how much rope does Clark have left?

5. At Tampa International Airport, 99 people board an airplane bound for Detroit Metro Airport. The plane makes one stop at Chicago O'Hare Airport. While stopped in Chicago, 62 people leave the plane and 20 people board the plane. About how many people are on the plane when it finally lands in Detroit?

6. Mr. Connolly bought hot dogs for a cookout at his school. On Monday, he grilled 120 hot dogs. On Wednesday, he grilled 231 hot dogs, and on Friday he grilled 160 hot dogs. About how many hot dogs did he cook in all?

HOME CONNECTION: UP FRONT

Dear Parent or Guardian:

Your child has been learning about front-end estimation. The activities have involved "buying" certain items that have certain prices and keeping a running total of the estimated total cost of the items so that a set amount of money will not be exceeded. Have your child accompany you on any ordinary shopping trip and fill in the Item column and the Front-End Cost column on this page. When you return home, help your child to record the actual costs of the items in the appropriate column. Talk with your child about how close his or her estimate of the total cost was to the store receipt's subtotal.

During a shopping trip, write the names of the items bought and a front-end estimate of the cost of each item. Find the total estimated cost. Then compare the estimated cost with the subtotal on the store receipt.

A Shopping Trip

Item	Actual Cost	Front-End Cost
Totals		

Name ______________________________

No Frowns in Town

THE BIGGEST FROWN IN TOWN

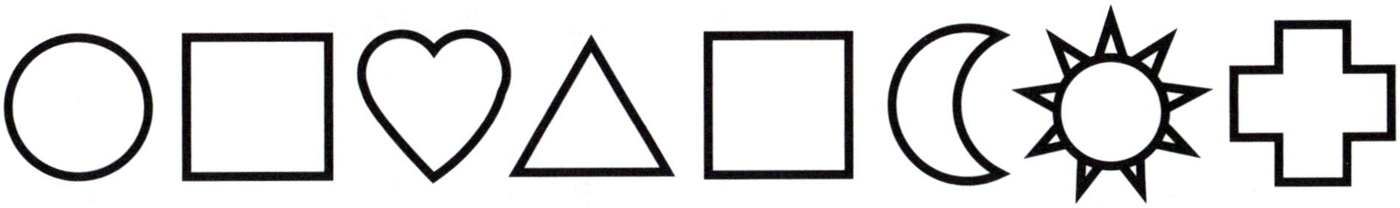

YOUR CHOICE

Which equation would you use to solve the problem? Circle the letter of the correct answer.

1. Jamie had 66 pieces of candy in a bowl. Six friends were coming to visit. How many pieces of candy will each friend receive?

   A $66 \div 6 = \square$ **C** $66 \times 6 = \square$

   B $6 + \square = 66$ **D** $66 + 6 = \square$

2. There are 26 apples on an apple tree. Rebecca picks some apples. There are 20 apples left on the tree. How many apples did Rebecca pick?

   F $20 + 26 = \square$ **H** $\square - 26 = 6$

   G $26 - \square = 20$ **I** $26 + \square = 32$

3. There are 3 cars and some trucks in a parking lot. There are 18 cars and trucks in all in the parking lot. Which equation shows how many trucks there are?

   A $18 \div 3 = \square$ **C** $18 + 3 = \square$

   B $3 \times \square = 18$ **D** $3 + \square = 18$

4. Marta asked 3 classmates to bring 24 cupcakes each to sell. Which equation shows the total number of cupcakes that the classmates are bringing?

   F $3 \times \square = 24$ **H** $3 + 24 = \square$

   G $\square \times 3 = 24$ **I** $3 \times 24 = \square$

5. Rory printed 50 posters. Meadow took some to place in stores. Rory had 20 posters left. How many posters did Meadow take?

   A $50 \div \square = 20$ **C** $50 - \square = 20$

   B $50 + \square = 20$ **D** $50 \times \square = 20$

6. Morgan bought a bookcase that had 5 shelves. He put 8 books on each shelf. How many books did Morgan put in his bookcase?

   F $5 + 8 = \square$ **H** $8 - 5 = \square$

   G $5 \times 8 = \square$ **I** $8 \div 5 = \square$

Name ____________________

BALANCING ACT

Solve each equation. Find the value that the variable stands for.

$6 + \square = 15$

$7 \times \square = 49$

$\square - 10 = 40$

$8 + \square = 24$

$10 \times \square = 60$

$\square \times 5 = 30$

$11 + 9 = \square$

$3 \times 4 = \square$

$18 - \square = 12$

WHAT'S THE PROBLEM?

Write a word problem for each equation. Make sure the equation can be used to solve the problem.

$6 + \square = 15$	$7 \times \square = 49$	$\square - 10 = 40$
$8 + \square = 24$	$10 \times \square = 60$	$\square \times 5 = 30$
$11 + 9 = \square$	$3 \times 4 = \square$	$18 - \square = 12$

Name ______________________________

HOME CONNECTION: WHAT'S THE NUMBER?

Dear Parent or Guardian:

Your child has been learning about variables, or unknown numbers, in expressions and in equations. The first exposure to unknowns has likely been an open square, or quad, that stands in for a number. In this lesson, your child has been learning that a symbol or letter can also be a variable in an expression or an equation. Your child has been learning to manipulate expressions and equations, using arithmetical operations, to find missing numbers. In this activity, your child will use as a reference the keypad for a telephone to find the missing numbers in telephone numbers.

Help your child to interpret the layout of the telephone keypad to find the sets of possible replacement numbers in each given telephone number on the reverse side of this page. The sum of the digits of each number is provided. Your child has to find the value of the variable in the telephone number that will produce the given sum.

- **Study the telephone keypad. Read the equation. The equation shows the sum of the seven digits in a telephone number. Identify the variable in the equation, and solve for it.**

Telephone Keypad

1	2 ABC	3 DEF
4 GHI	5 JKL	6 MNO
7 PRS	8 TUV	9 WXY
*	0	#

Solve for the variable in the equation. Write the letters or the number of the keypad button that has the number that is the value of the variable.

1. 787-54*n*3 = 38

   $n =$

2. 542-*n*576 = 30

   $n =$

3. 6*n*6-4895 = 45

   $n =$

4. 415-*n*854 = 36

   $n =$

Name ______________________________

Modeling Decimals

TAKE YOUR PLACES

Place-Value Chart

Tens	Ones		Tenths
		•	
		•	
		•	
		•	
		•	
		•	
		•	
		•	
		•	
		•	
		•	
		•	
		•	
		•	
		•	
		•	
		•	
		•	
		•	
		•	

A PLACE OF MY OWN

Place-Value Chart

Tens	Ones		Tenths	Hundredths
		.		
		.		
		.		
		.		
		.		
		.		
		.		
		.		
		.		
		.		
		.		
		.		
		.		
		.		
		.		
		.		
		.		
		.		
		.		
		.		

Name ______________________________

MODELING TENTHS

If the decimal is pictured, write it in the place-value chart. If the decimal is in the place-value chart, draw a picture of it. Hint: 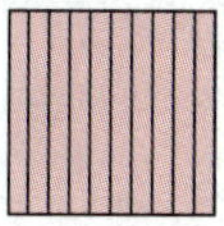 = 1, and  = one tenth.

1. Example: 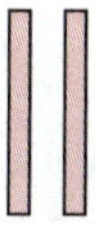

Tens	Ones	and	Tenths
	0	.	2

2.

Tens	Ones	and	Tenths
	0	.	7

3. 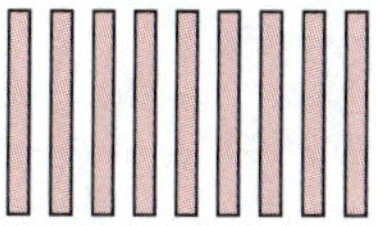

Tens	Ones	and	Tenths
		.	

4.

Tens	Ones	and	Tenths
	0	.	1

5.

Tens	Ones	and	Tenths
	1	.	5

6. 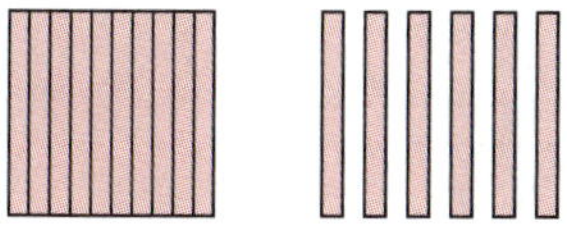

Tens	Ones	and	Tenths
		.	

7.

Tens	Ones	and	Tenths
	1	.	0

8.

Tens	Ones	and	Tenths
	0	.	3

MODELING HUNDREDTHS

If the decimal is pictured, write it in the place-value chart.
If the decimal is in the place-value chart, draw a picture of it. Hint: 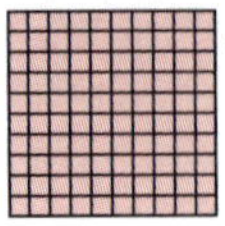 = 1,  = one tenth, = one hundredth.

1. Example:

Tens	Ones	and	Tenths	Hundredths
	0	.	0	3

2.

Tens	Ones	and	Tenths	Hundredths
	0	.	0	5

3. 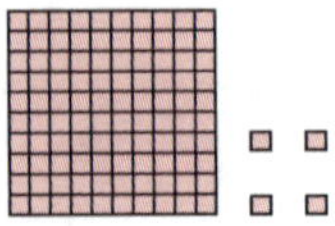

Tens	Ones	and	Tenths	Hundredths
		.		

4. 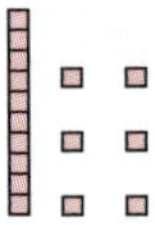

Tens	Ones	and	Tenths	Hundredths
		.		

5.

Tens	Ones	and	Tenths	Hundredths
	1	.	2	3

6. 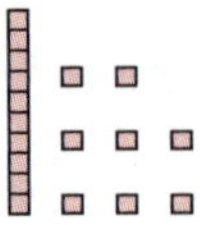

Tens	Ones	and	Tenths	Hundredths
		.		

7.

Tens	Ones	and	Tenths	Hundredths
	0	.	3	5

8.

Tens	Ones	and	Tenths	Hundredths
	0	.	0	7

Name ____________________

DECIMAL MATCH GAME

0.4	0.1	1	0.2	0.9	0.5
four tenths	one tenth	one whole	two tenths	nine tenths	five tenths
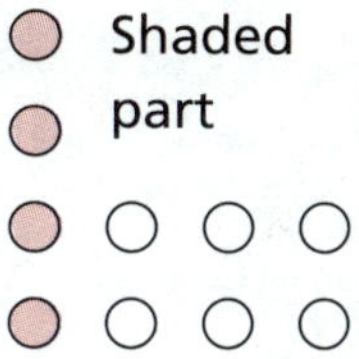 Shaded part	 Shaded part	 Shaded part	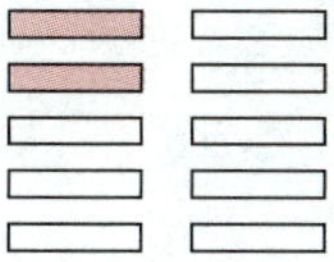 Shaded part	 Shaded part	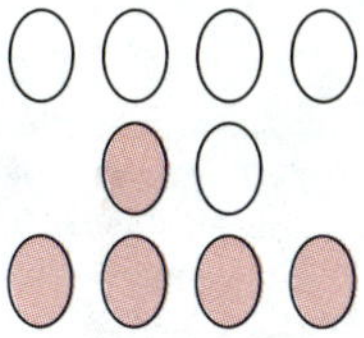 Shaded part
Ms. Crocker cut the cake into 10 pieces. 4 of the pieces had candles on them. How many tenths had candles?	$\frac{1}{10}$	Lucinda ate the entire muffin by herself. What part of the muffin did she eat?	Mickey had a pack of 10 baseball cards. He gave 2 cards to a friend. How many tenths did he give away?	Arn and his friends ate 9 pieces of pizza. One piece remained. How many tenths did they eat?	Patty and Allie made 10 ice pops. They ate half of them. How many tenths remained?
0.3	0.6	0.7	0.8	$\frac{3}{10}$	Will saw ants in the dog's dish! He saw 4 on the food. 6 ran from the dish. How many tenths ran from the dish?
three tenths	six tenths	seven tenths	eight tenths	Alf and Ralph tried to eat 10 hot dogs. They ate 7 of them. How many tenths were left?	Bill bought 10 ice pops. 8 of them are cherry and 2 are lime. How many tenths are cherry?
Tally Points **Player 1:** **Player 2:**	$\frac{6}{10}$	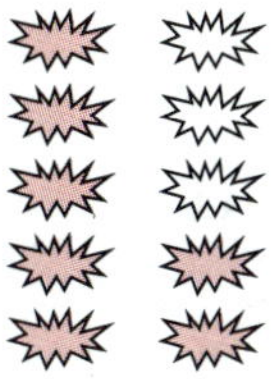	$\frac{8}{10}$	Chucky took 10 toys to the beach. 3 toys floated away. How many toys remained?	

Name ______________________________

HOME CONNECTION: DECIMAL MATCH GAME

Dear Parent or Guardian:

Your child has been learning how to identify decimals and money amounts using graphic models. He or she has brought home the cards for the Decimal Match Game. (If your child does not have the cards, you can cut out the cards on the next page.) Please play the game with your child.

How to play Decimal Match Game:

- Place the 40 playing cards facedown on the floor or on a table. You may wish to use an 8×5 or 10×4 grid.

- The point of the game is to find pairs of cards with matching values, such as "two tenths" and "0.2." Matches can be decimals, fractions, models, or word phrases that have the same value. **Note:** There are 2 pairs of matching cards for each tenth from 0.1 through 1.

- Player 1 turns over two cards. If the cards are a match, Player 1 keeps the cards and flips over two more cards. If the cards do not match, Player 1 returns the cards to their original facedown positions. The turn then switches to Player 2. When all cards have been matched, the player with the most cards wins the game.

- You can reshuffle the cards and play again, if you'd like.

DECIMAL MATCH GAME

0.4	0.1	1	0.2	0.9	0.5
four tenths	one tenth	one whole	two tenths	nine tenths	five tenths
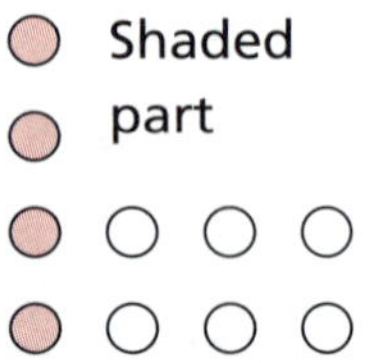 Shaded part	 Shaded part	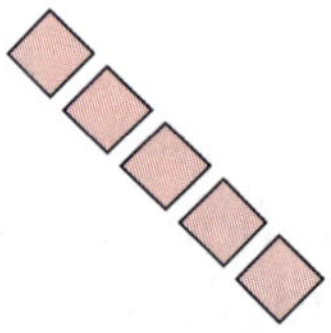 Shaded part	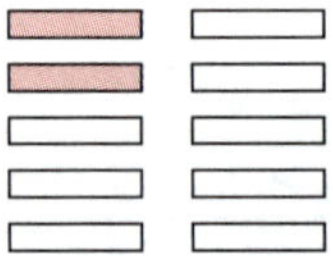 Shaded part	 Shaded part	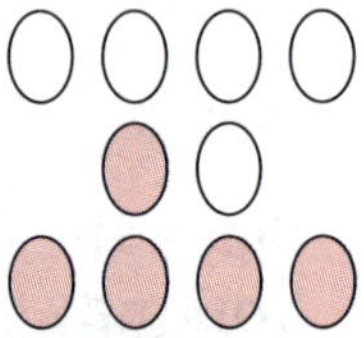 Shaded part
Ms. Crocker cut the cake into 10 pieces. 4 of the pieces had candles on them. How many tenths had candles?	$\frac{1}{10}$	Lucinda ate the entire muffin by herself. What part of the muffin did she eat?	Mickey had a pack of 10 baseball cards. He gave 2 cards to a friend. How many tenths did he give away?	Arn and his friends ate 9 pieces of pizza. One piece remained. How many tenths did they eat?	Patty and Allie made 10 ice pops. They ate half of them. How many tenths remained?
0.3	0.6	0.7	0.8	$\frac{3}{10}$	Will saw ants in the dog's dish! He saw 4 on the food. 6 ran from the dish. How many tenths ran from the dish?
three tenths	six tenths	seven tenths	eight tenths	Alf and Ralph tried to eat 10 hot dogs. They ate 7 of them. How many tenths were left?	Bill bought 10 ice pops. 8 of them are cherry and 2 are lime. How many tenths are cherry?
Tally Points **Player 1:** **Player 2:**	$\frac{6}{10}$	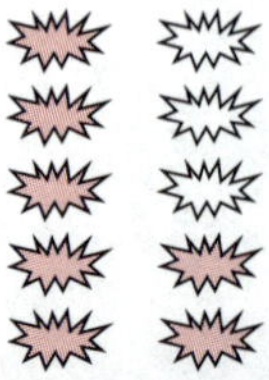	$\frac{8}{10}$	Chucky took 10 toys to the beach. 3 toys floated away. How many toys remained?	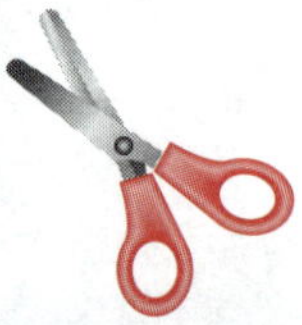

TOPIC 3
Geomeasure I

Name ______________________________

By Leaps and Bounds

MEASURING STUFF AROUND THE ROOM

1. What is the perimeter of your desk measured in centimeters? (Use a metric tape measure.)

2. How many jumbo paper clips long is the perimeter of your desk?

3. What is the width of your classroom doorway measured in meters? (Use a meterstick.)

4. How many pieces of string long is the width of your doorway?

5. How many paces is it from the front of your classroom to the back of your classroom?

6. How many meters is it from the front of your classroom to the back of your classroom? (Use a meterstick or a trundle wheel.)

7. How many inches wide is your desk? (Use a ruler.)

8. What is the width of your classroom measured in feet? (Use a ruler or a yardstick.)

WHICH IS SHORTEST?

Use any methods or tools that you like to find out which is the shortest route from Jack's house to Rapunzel's castle.

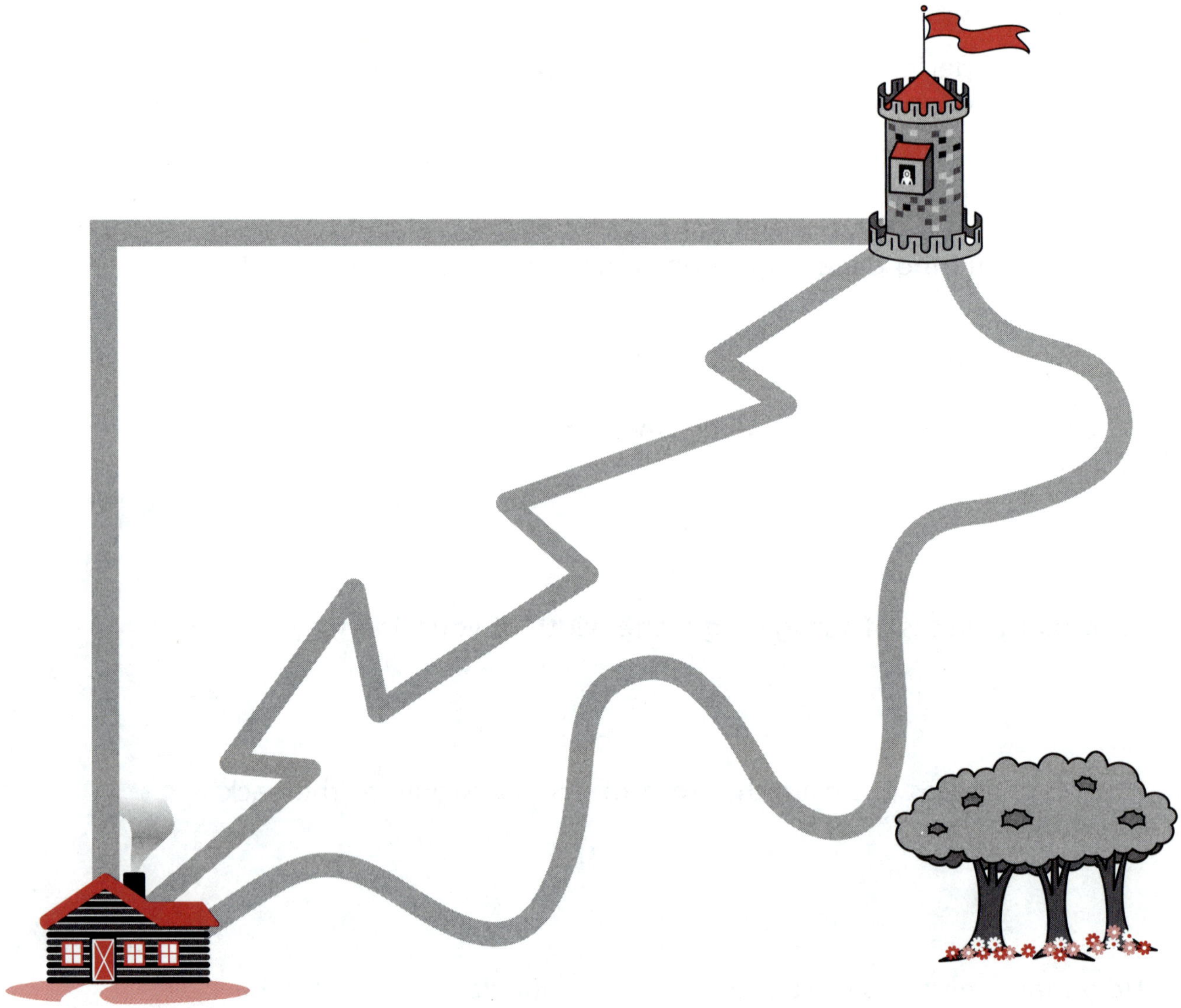

Which path is shortest? How did you find out?

____

____

____

Name ______________________

HOW CLOSE CAN YOU GET? (A)

	Which referent did you use?	How many referent units was the item?	Which standard unit would you use to measure the item?	What is your estimate in standard units?	What was the actual measurement in standard units?	What was the difference between the estimate and the actual length?
Width of your math book						
Distance from your class to the cafeteria						
Height of your desk						
Length of a chalkboard in class						

HOW CLOSE CAN YOU GET? (B)

	Which referent did you use?	How many referent units was the item?	Which standard unit would you use to measure the item?	What is your estimate in standard units?	What was the actual measurement in standard units?	What was the difference between the estimate and the actual length?
Length of the chalkboard eraser						
Distance from sink to door						
Distance from class door to office door						
Length of the bulletin board						

Name ______________________________

HOME CONNECTION: ON FOOT

Dear Parent or Guardian:

Your child has been learning how to use nonstandard measures, such as a pace, to estimate length. Have your child follow the directions on the following page to find which of two nearby locations is closer to your home. You may want to supervise your child as he or she completes this activity.

- Choose two locations that you think are about the same distance from your home, such as nearby stores or friends' homes.

- Count the number of paces you take to reach each location.

- Then compare the distances, to find out which location is closer to your home.

Location A ______________________________

Number of paces from home ______________________________

Location B ______________________________

Number of paces from home ______________________________

Which of the two locations is closer to your home? ______________________________

Name ______________________________

The Shape of Things to Come

POLYGONS AND OTHER FIGURES

A polygon is a closed figure.
A polygon is made only of line segments.
A polygon's line segments meet only at their endpoints.

1. Circle the figures that are polygons.

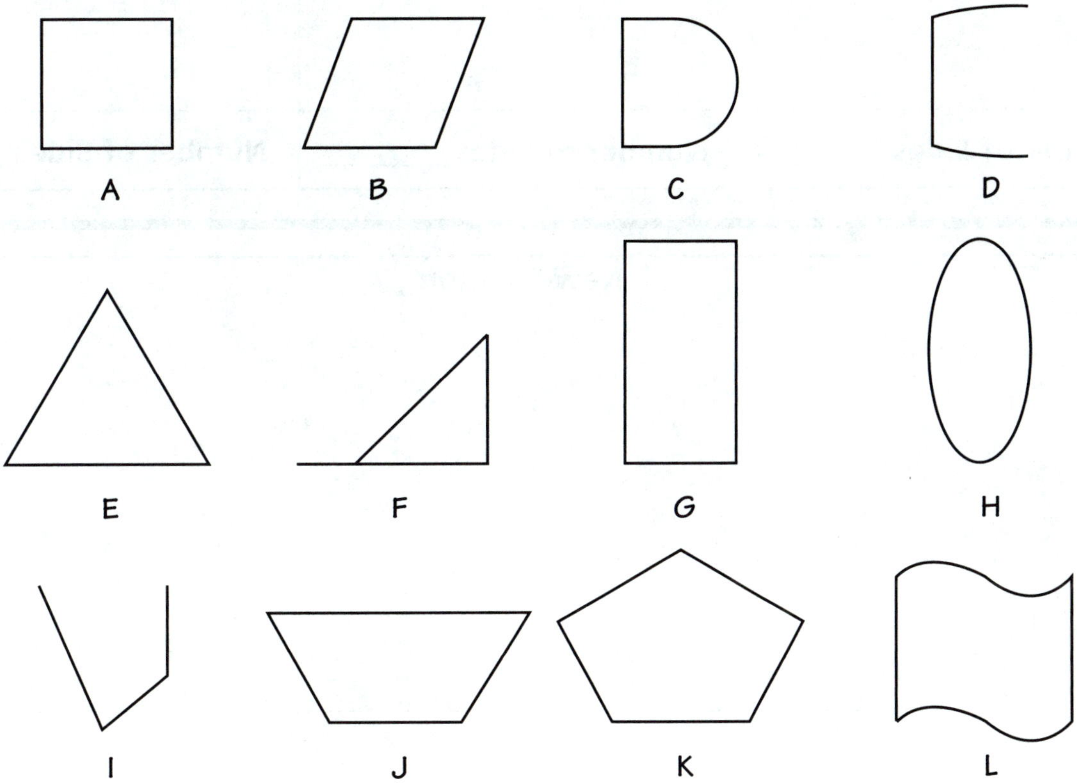

Complete the sentence.

2. Figure F is not a polygon because ______________________________

____

3. Figure H is not a polygon because ______________________________

____

4. Figure I is not a polygon because ______________________________

____

CREATE YOUR OWN POLYGONS

Choose three pattern blocks and arrange them to create your own polygon. Only align congruent sides of the blocks. Then answer the questions.

First Block	Second Block	Third Block
Number of Sides _______	**Number of Sides** _______	**Number of Sides** _______

New Polygon	
Type of Polygon ____________________	**Number of Sides** ____________________

1. What is the total number of sides of your three blocks?

2. How many sides does your new polygon have?

3. Does your new polygon have more sides or fewer sides than the total of the three blocks?

Name ____

HOME CONNECTION: PORTRAIT WITH POLYGONS

Dear Parent or Guardian:

Your child has been learning about polygons and their attributes. A polygon is a closed figure made only of line segments that meet only at their endpoints. Squares and triangles are polygons; lines and circles are not. With your help, your child will draw a picture using as many polygons as possible. Encourage your child to be creative. Ask your child to show you the polygons in his or her picture.

Draw a picture using as many polygons as possible. Be creative! Your brother could be a triangle; a peanut-butter sandwich could be a rhombus.

triangle	quadrilateral	pentagon
hexagon	heptagon	octagon
square	equilateral triangle	right triangle
regular polygon	rhombus	

Name ______________________________

The Mysterious Polygonians

THE POLYGONIAN ALPHABET

Follow your teacher's instructions. Use straws, tape, and clay to make the polygonian letter. Then draw it and complete the list of its attributes.

English Letter	Polygonian Letter	Geometrical Name	Attributes
A	•	point	• A point is a location. • A point has no _________.
B		line	• A line is an endless straight set of _________. • A line extends in _________ directions.
C		line segment	• A line segment is part of a _________. • A line segment has _________ endpoints.
D		ray	• A ray is part of a _________. • A ray has _________endpoint. • A ray extends forever in one direction.
E		angle	• An angle is a figure formed by two rays with the same _________. • The endpoint is called the angle's _________.

English Letter	Polygonian Letter	Geometrical Name	Attributes
G		right angle	• A right angle forms a ________ corner. • You can use the symbol ⌝ to show a right angle.
H		intersecting lines	• Intersecting lines are lines that ________.
I		parallel lines	• Parallel lines are lines that never ______________.
K		perpendicular lines	• Perpendicular lines are lines that intersect and form ________ right angles.
L		congruent line segments	• Congruent line segments are the same ________.
M		triangle	• A triangle is a polygon with ________ sides and ________ vertices.

Name ______________________________

English Letter	Polygonian Letter	Geometrical Name	Attributes
N		quadrilateral	• A quadrilateral is a polygon with ________ sides and ________ vertices.
O		trapezoid	• A trapezoid is a quadrilateral with ________, and only ________, pair of parallel sides
P		parallelogram	• A parallelogram is a quadrilateral with ________ pairs of parallel sides. • The parallel sides are also ____________.
R		rectangle	• A rectangle is a parallelogram. • A rectangle has ________ right angles.
S		rhombus	• A rhombus is a parallelogram. • A rhombus has ________ congruent sides.

English Letter	Polygonian Letter	Geometrical Name	Attributes
T		square	• A square is a rhombus. • A square has __________ right angles. • So a square is also a ________________.
U		pentagon	• A pentagon has __________ sides and __________ vertices.
V		hexagon	• A hexagon has __________ sides and __________ vertices.
W		heptagon	• A heptagon has __________ sides and __________ vertices.
Y		octagon	• An octagon has __________ sides and __________ vertices.

Name ____

MYSTERIOUS POLYGONIAN MESSAGES

In the vast Heptagonia Desert, archaeolgists have discovered several stones with messages written in the Polygonian alphabet. The archaeologists have already translated the messages of one stone, a series of questions. Now they have found the stone with the answers!

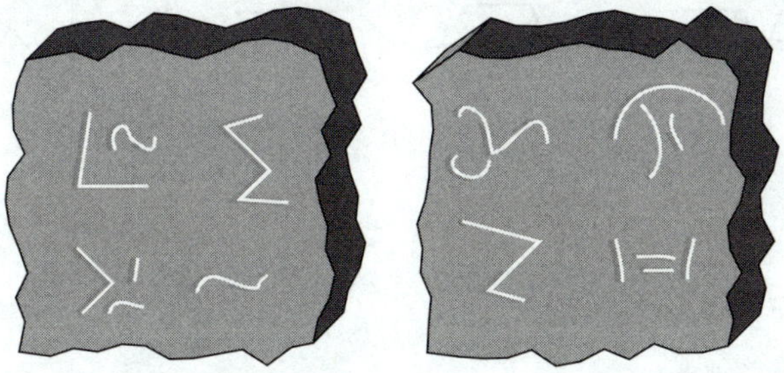

Use your knowledge of the Polygonian alphabet to translate the answers to these ancient questions.

1. What do you call it when two bad rays get together?

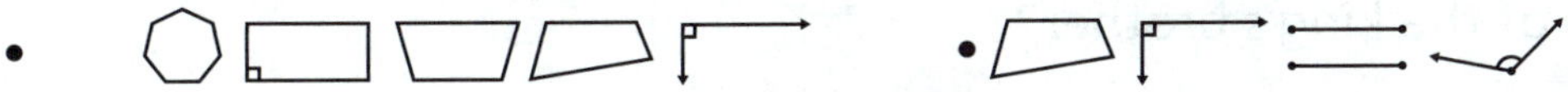

2. What do acorns say when they grow up?

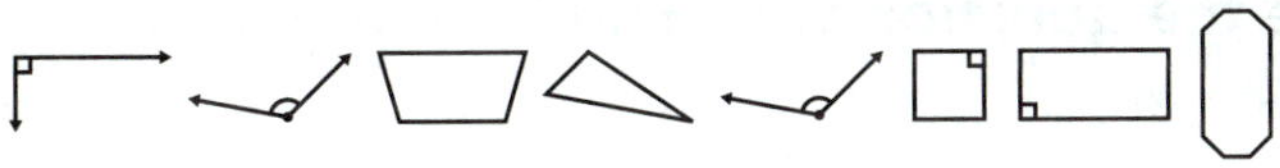

3. When lines want to meet, where do they go?

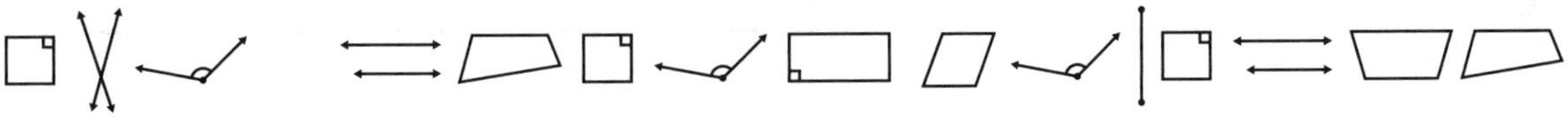

4. What became of the the square that the king sat upon?

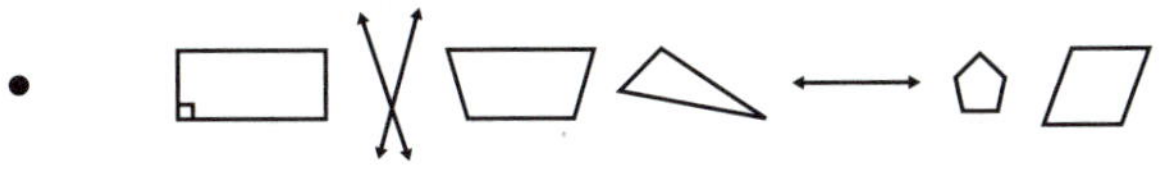

5. What did the queen say when her parrot flew away?

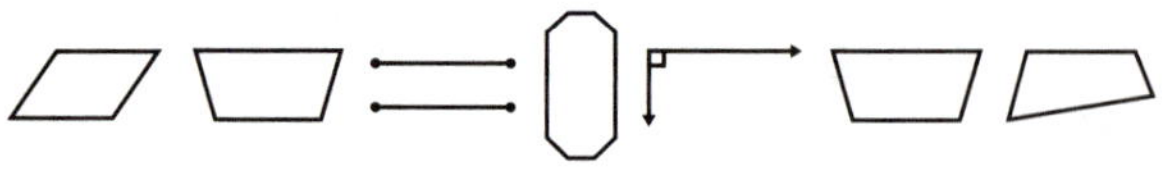

6. What part of a line can't you trust?

7. What is the king's name?

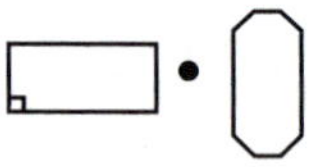

8. What is the name of the king's brother?

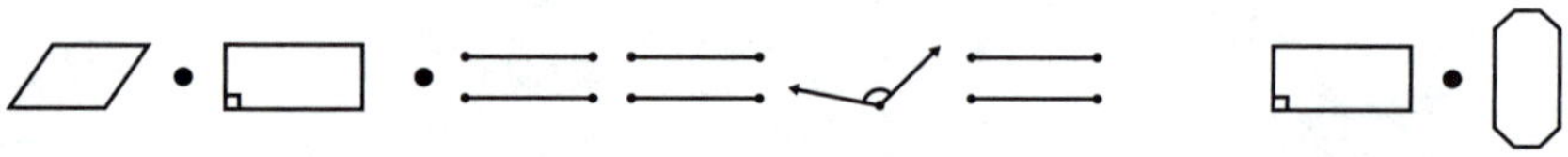

Invent your own Polygonian riddle. Write the question with English letters. Write the answer with Polygonian letters.

9. Question: ______________________________

____

Answer: ______________________________

____

10. Question: ______________________________

____

Answer: ______________________________

____

Name ______________________________

HOME CONNECTION: POLYGONS AT HOME

Dear Parent or Guardian:

Your child has been learning about geometric figures (such as lines, rays, and angles) and polygons (such as triangles, rectangles, and pentagons). In this assignment, your child will find examples of these figures and polygons in your home. For example, the corner of a door could represent an angle, while two adjoining sides of a tile could represent perpendicular lines.

Draw or describe an example of the figure or polygon.

1. point

2. line

3. line segment

4. angle

5. right angle

6. intersecting lines

7. parallel lines

8. perpendicular lines

9. congruent line segments

10. triangle

11. trapezoid

12. parallelogram

13. rectangle

14. rhombus

15. square

16. pentagon

17. hexagon

18. octagon

Name ______________________________

Area and Perimeter Man

MY PICTURE SQUARES

Name ______________________________

MEASURE US

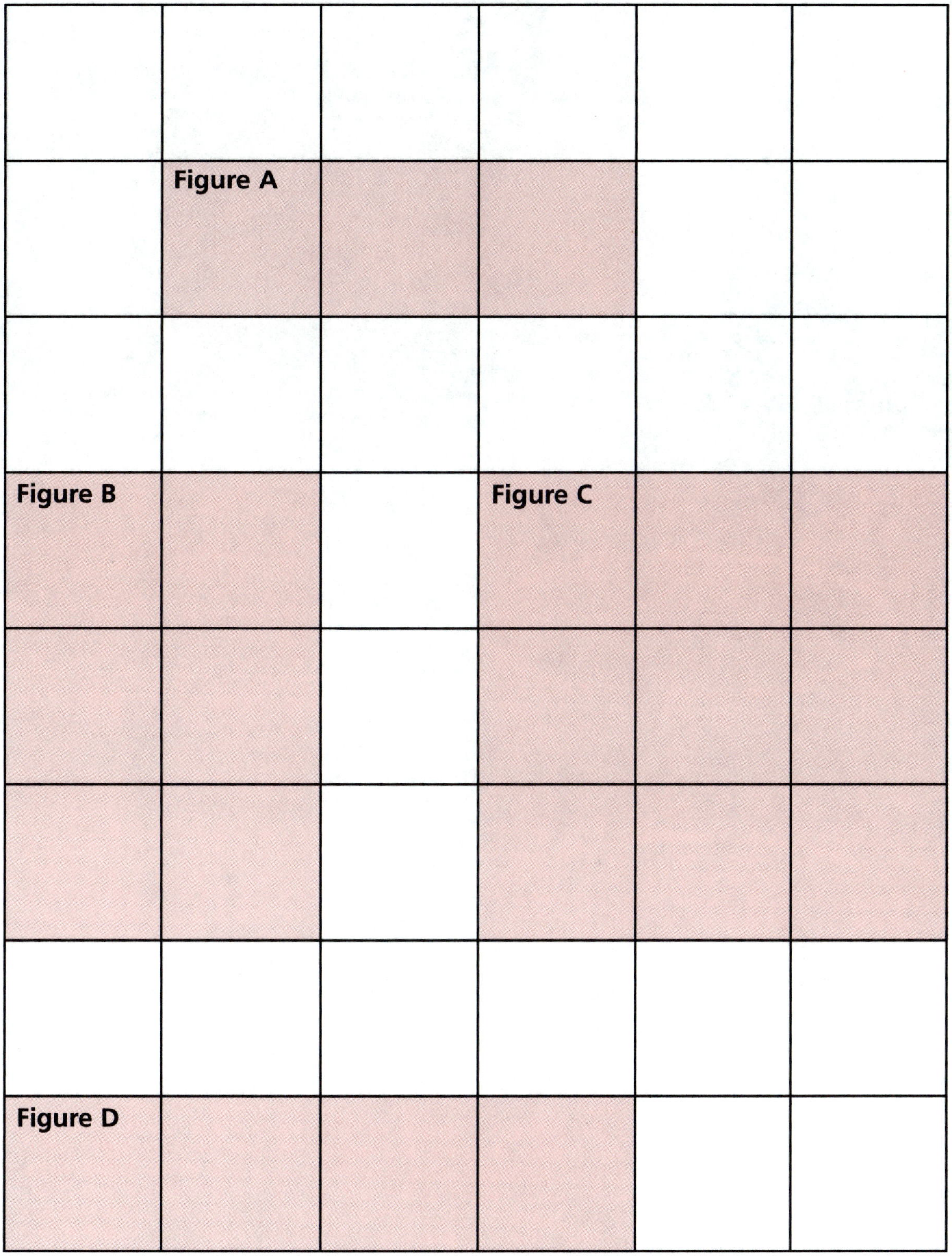

DRAW THE MEASURES

Name ____________________

NO SQUARES HERE

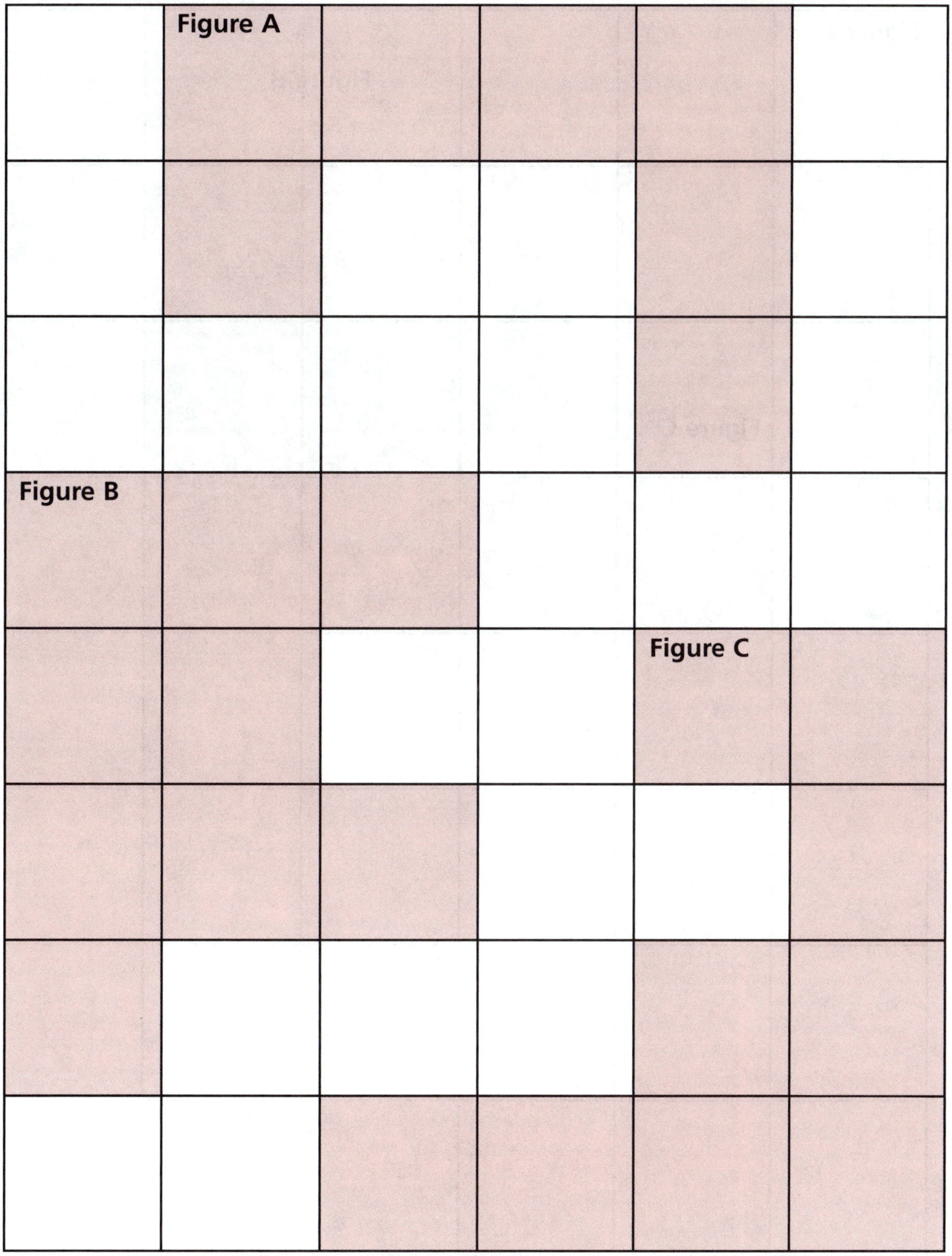

IT'S ABOUT THIS SIZE

Estimate the perimeter and area of each figure.

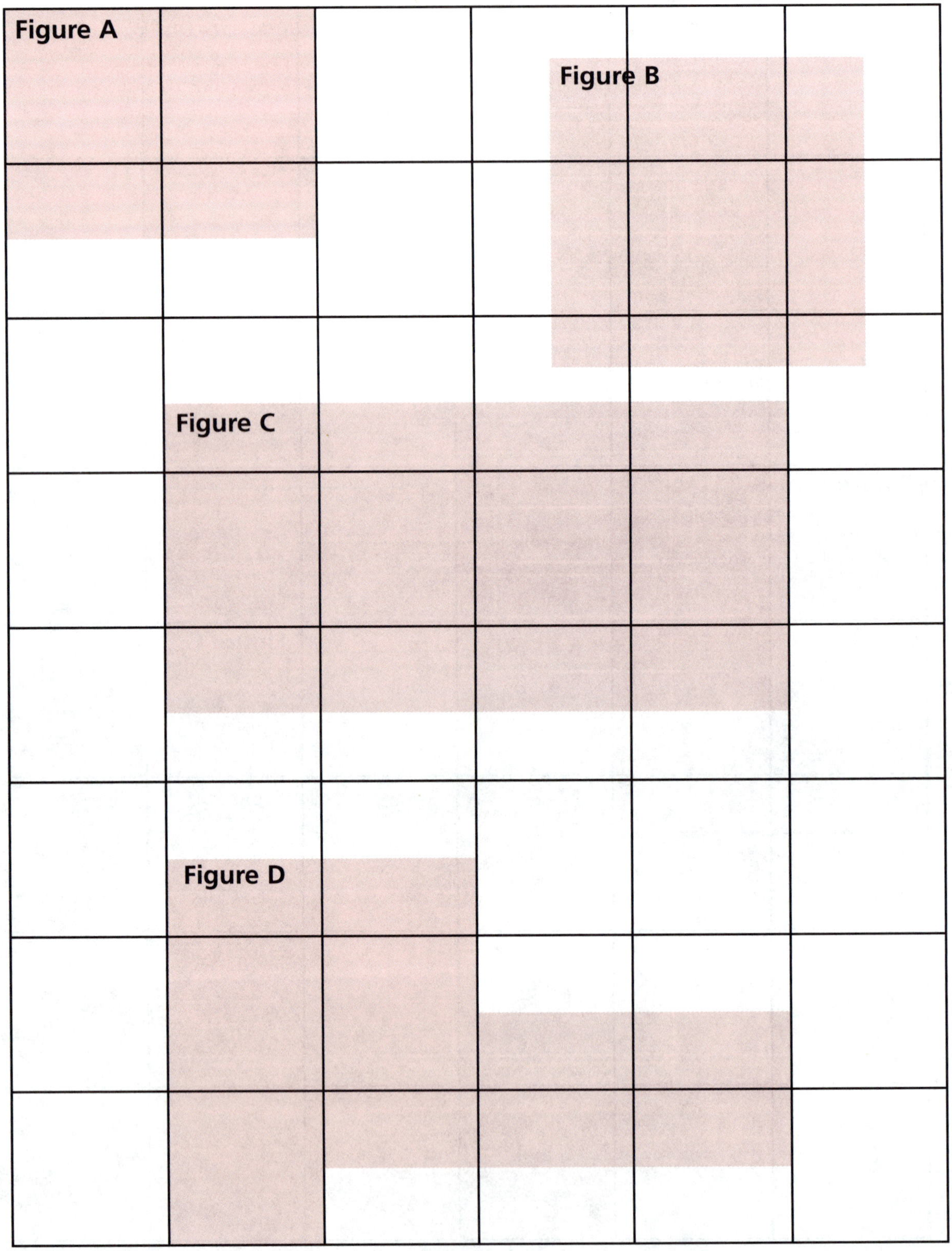

Name____

HOME CONNECTION: MEASURE UP!

Dear Parent or Guardian:

Your child has been learning how to find areas and perimeters. To do so, he or she has been drawing figures on grid paper and finding the area of each figure by counting the squares within it. Here is an example of how your child has been using counting to find area and perimeter:

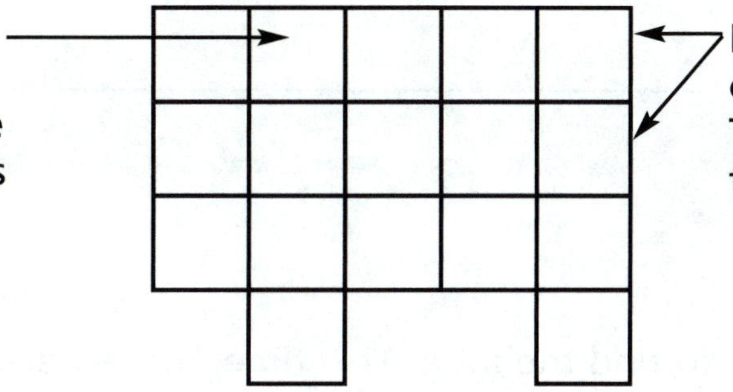

Area is found by counting the squares inside the figure. The area is 17 square units.

Perimeter is found by counting the sides. The perimeter of this figure is 20 units.

Now, your child is going to find the area and perimeter of a table in your home, using this page as a measuring tool.

You can help your child while participating in his or her learning experience. Because your child will be using only this page to measure the perimeter and area, he or she will have to move it around the surface of the table and count the number of pages. You can help your child keep track of the number of "pages" it takes to measure the perimeter and cover the area. If you have extra notebook paper in your home, your child could use it to cover the table and then just count the sheets to find the area.

If not intrusive, your child can also use the page to find the perimeter of a room in your home.

Measure the Perimeter

- Use this page to measure the perimeter and area of a table in your home.
- First lay the page lengthwise along the edge at one corner of the table. Place your finger along the edge where the page ends. Then flip the page over your finger. Be careful to keep the page along the edge.
- When you get to the next corner, turn the page lengthwise and move down the next side.
- Move around the table this way and count each time you flip the page. When you get back to where you started, the number you have counted will be the perimeter.

The perimeter of my table is ______________________________

Measure the Area

- You can also use the page to find the area. This time, move back and forth across the table from one end to the other. The point is to find out how many pages it takes to cover the table.

The area of my table is ______________________________

Use the page to measure the perimeter and area of other surfaces in your home. Use the space below to record the measurements.

Name ______________________________

Weight Up

THIS OBJECT WEIGHS...

Write the unit of measure from the word bank that you would use to weigh each object.

Word Bank		
ounce	pound	ton

1. Large school book ______________________
2. A loaf of bread ______________________
3. Ten quarters ______________________
4. A goldfish ______________________
5. A school bus full of kids ______________________
6. A bicycle ______________________
7. An apple ______________________
8. A wooden ruler ______________________
9. A power lawnmower ______________________
10. A large mobile home ______________________

ESTIMATE AND WEIGH

Station	Referent	Weight of Referent	Item to Estimate	My Estimate	Measured Weight	Difference between "my estimate" and "measured weight"
Example	Paperback book	5 ounces	Grapefruit	6 ounces	8 ounces	2 ounces
1						
2						
3						
4						
5						
6						
7						
8						
9						
10						

Name ______________________________

HOME CONNECTION: HOW MUCH DOES IT WEIGH?

Dear Parent or Guardian:

Your child has been learning how to estimate the weights of objects and how to choose the appropriate unit, including ounce, pound, and ton. In class, your child has held different items, such as an eraser and a paper clip, to determine if the item weighed more or less than an ounce. He or she has also determined whether classroom objects, such as a desk, would be weighed in ounces, pounds, or tons.

In this activity, your child will choose objects around the home, list them on the reverse side of this page, and write whether the object would be weighed in ounces, pounds, or tons. You can participate in the activity by choosing objects around your home for your child to use. Obviously, things that weigh a ton are limited, so you might point out a car, truck, or other vehicle for your child to use for his or her drawing.

Choose items around your home that weigh ounces, pounds, and tons. Write the name of the item in the appropriate category.

Ounces	Less than 1 Pound	More than 1 Pound

Draw a picture of something around your home or neighborhood that weighs a ton.

Name ____

Piping Hot

IMPORTANT TEMPERATURES

Read the thermometer to answer the question.

1. What temperature does the thermometer show in degrees Fahrenheit?
2. What temperature does the thermometer show in degrees Celsius?
3. At what temperature in degrees Fahrenheit does water boil?
4. At what temperature in degrees Celsius does water boil?
5. If your body temperature is 101°F, do you have a fever?
6. Would you wear a coat and scarf on a day with a temperature of 35°C?
7. At what temperature in degrees Celsius does water freeze?
8. At what temperature in degrees Fahrenheit does water freeze?
9. What was the temperature in degrees Fahrenheit in Death Valley on July 10, 1913?
10. Would you go for a swim at the beach on a day with a temperature of 90°F?

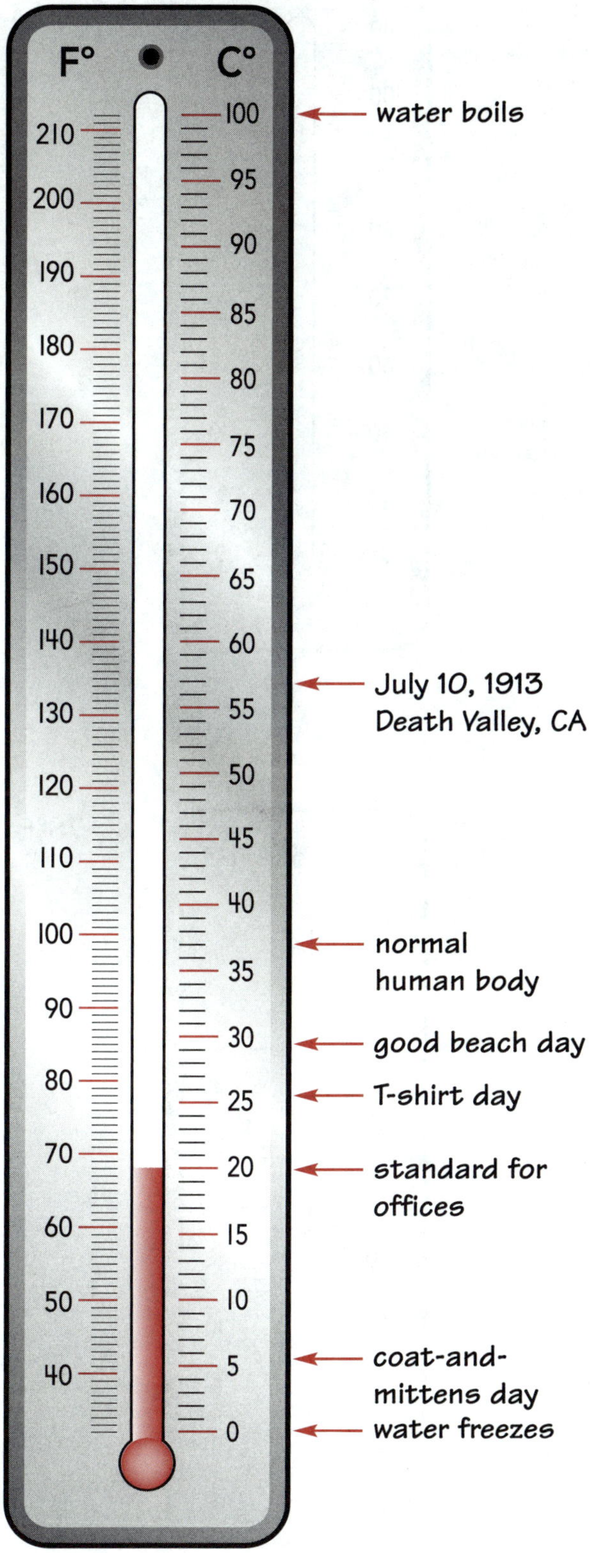

THERMOMETERS

Shade the thermometer to show the temperature.

1. 40°F

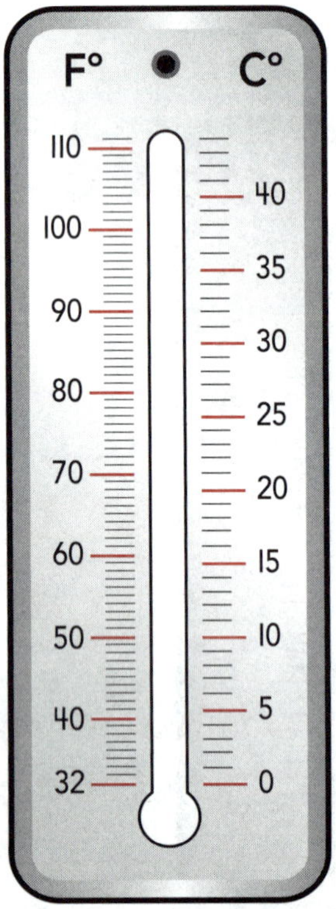

2. 40°C

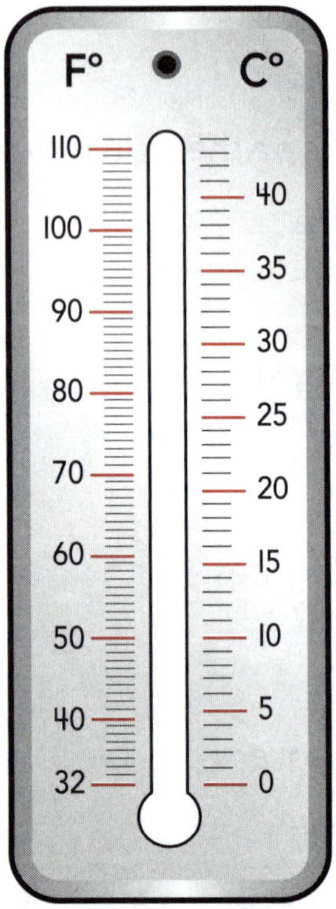

3. 26°C

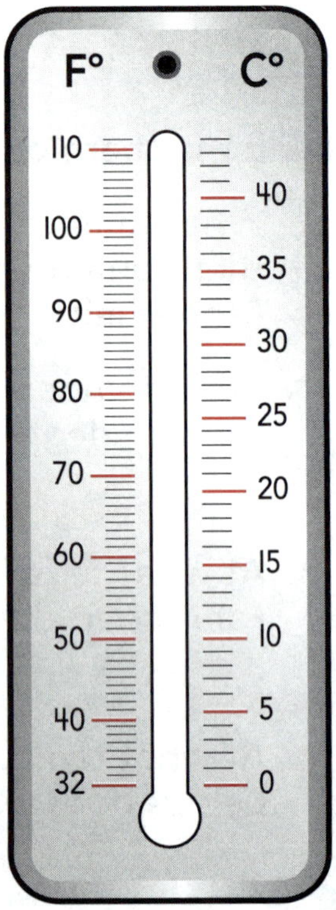

4. 101°F

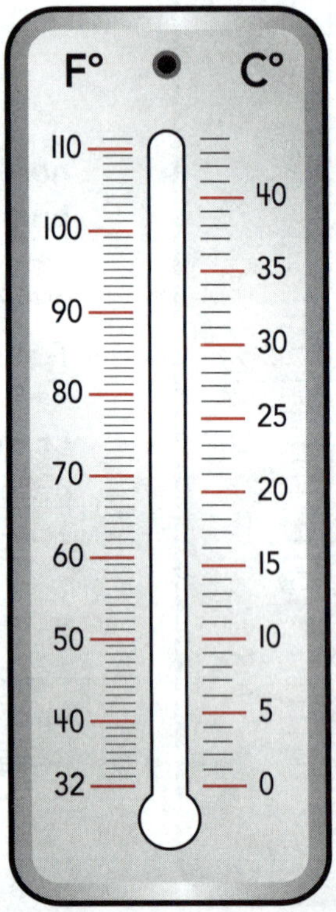

5. 78°F

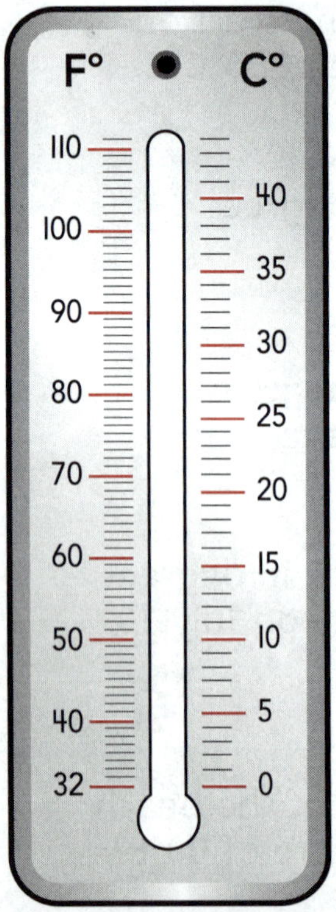

6. 5°C

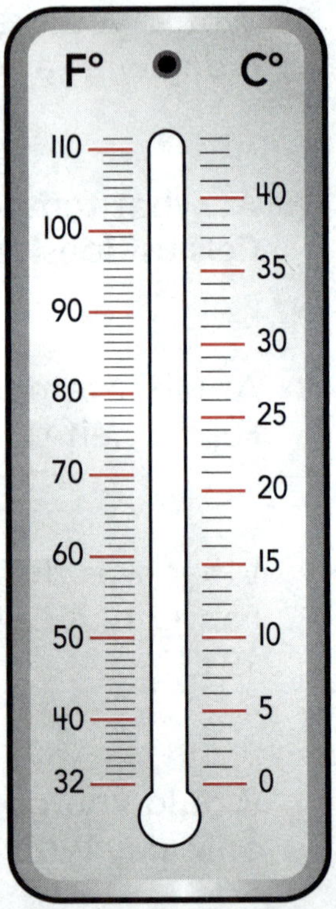

Name ____________________

Use the thermometers in problems 1–6 to answer the question.

7. Which temperature is hotter—40°F or 40°C?

8. What is the difference between 40°C and 26°C?

   degrees Celsius

9. What is the difference between 101°F and 78°F?

   degrees Fahrenheit

10. The temperature was 5°C. Then it rose 9 degrees Celsius. What was the new temperature?

11. The temperature was 40°F. Then it rose 37 degrees Fahrenheit. What was the new temperature?

12. Which two thermometers on page 112 most likely show the temperature of summer days?

    thermometer number ____ and thermometer number ____

13. Which two thermometers most likely show the temperature of winter days?

    thermometer number ____ and thermometer number ____

Solve the problem.

14. The temperature is 90°F. What is the approximate temperature in degrees Celsius?

    about

15. The temperature is 21°C. What is the approximate temperature in degrees Fahrenheit?

    about

16. A student did a chemical experiment. At first, the chemical was 38°C. Then its temperature dropped 25 degrees Celsius. What was the new temperature?

17. A motor was 108°F. After running for a while, its temperature rose 56 degrees Fahrenheit. What was its new temperature?

GOLDENLOCKS'S OATMEAL EXPERIMENT

Follow your teacher's instructions to help perform the experiment. Record the temperature data in the table. Use the data to answer the question.

My prediction: ______________________________________

Oatmeal Temperatures

Elapsed Time	Fred Bear's Oatmeal (1 package)	Mrs. Bear's Oatmeal (2 packages)	Mr. Bear's Oatmeal (4 packages)
1 minute			
3 minutes			
5 minutes			
7 minutes			
9 minutes			
11 minutes			
13 minutes			
15 minutes			

1. How much cooler than the boiling temperature of water was Fred's oatmeal at 1 minute?

2. How long did it take Mr. Bear's oatmeal to cool to 110°F?

3. How long did it take Mrs. Bear's oatmeal to cool to 110°F?

4. How long did it take Fred's oatmeal to cool to 110°F?

5. If Goldenlocks was in a hurry, whose oatmeal was she most likely to have had time to eat?

Name ______________________________

HOME CONNECTION: HIGH AND LOW

Dear Parent or Guardian:

Your child has been learning about temperature. He or she has learned how to read a thermometer, finding temperatures in degrees Fahrenheit and in degrees Celsius. For this assignment, your child will record high and low outside temperatures for three days. Then your child will find the difference between each day's high and low temperatures. If you don't have an outside thermometer, your child can find the temperatures on the weather page of a newspaper.

Record the high temperature and the low temperature each day for three days. You can use a thermometer or find the temperatures on the weather page of a newspaper. Find the difference of the temperatures for each day. Which day had the greatest range of temperatures?

Day 1

High temperature: ____________________

Low temperature: ____________________

Difference: ____________________

Day 2

High temperature: ____________________

Low temperature: ____________________

Difference: ____________________

Day 3

High temperature: ____________________

Low temperature: ____________________

Difference: ____________________

The day with the greatest range of temperatures was ____________________

Name ____

Capacity Comparison

NO SPLASHING, PLEASE!

Follow your teacher's instructions. Use measuring tools and water—no splashing, please!—to answer the question.

1. How many cups are there in 1 quart? cups
2. How many quarts are there in 1 gallon? quarts
3. How many cups are there in 1 pint? cups
4. How many pints are there in 1 gallon? pints
5. How many pints are there in 1 quart? pints
6. How many cups are there in 1 gallon? cups
7. How many pints are there in 2 quarts? pints
8. How many quart containers can be filled with 8 cups?
   quart containers
9. How many gallon containers can be filled with 24 pints?
   gallon containers
10. How many pint containers can be filled with 12 cups?
    pint containers
11. What fraction of a gallon container can be filled with 2 quarts?
    of a gallon container
12. What fraction of a gallon container can be filled with 4 cups?
    of a gallon container
13. What fraction of a quart container can be filled with 3 cups?
    of a quart container
14. Write the customary units of capacity in order from largest to smallest.

THE FUNDAMENTALS

Shade equivalent sections of the chart and write the missing measure.
The letter *c* means cup.

1. 1 quart = ____ cups

gallon	=	quart	quart	=	pint	pint	=	c	c	c	c
					pint	pint		c	c	c	c
		quart	quart		pint	pint		c	c	c	c
					pint	pint		c	c	c	c

2. 12 cups = ____ pints

gallon	=	quart	quart	=	pint	pint	=	c	c	c	c
					pint	pint		c	c	c	c
		quart	quart		pint	pint		c	c	c	c
					pint	pint		c	c	c	c

3. ____ pints = 1 gallon

gallon	=	quart	quart	=	pint	pint	=	c	c	c	c
					pint	pint		c	c	c	c
		quart	quart		pint	pint		c	c	c	c
					pint	pint		c	c	c	c

4. ____ quarts = 4 pints

gallon	=	quart	quart	=	pint	pint	=	c	c	c	c
					pint	pint		c	c	c	c
		quart	quart		pint	pint		c	c	c	c
					pint	pint		c	c	c	c

Name ______________________________

TABLES OF EQUIVALENCE

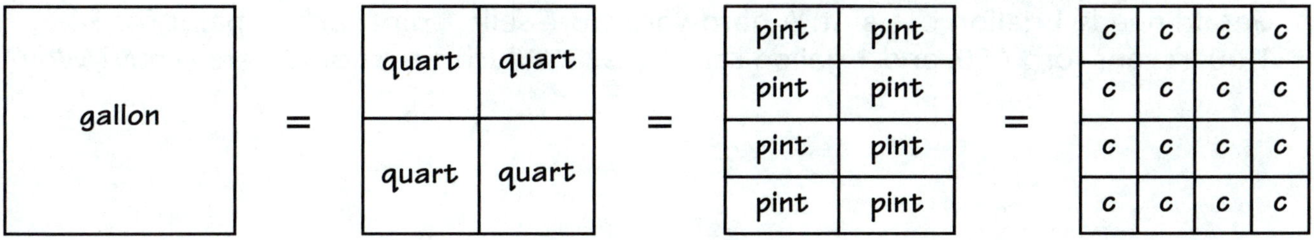

Complete the table to find the equivalent measure.

1. How many quarts are needed to fill 6 gallon containers? ______ quarts

gallon	1	2	3			
quarts	4	8				

2. How many cups are needed to fill 5 pint containers? ______ cups

pints	1				

3. How many pints are needed to fill 7 quart containers? ______ pints

4. How many cups are needed to fill 3 gallon containers? ______ cups

5. How many pints are needed to fill 6 gallon containers? ______ pints

CAPACITY CONUNDRUMS

Solve. Explain your answer.

1. Gerald needs 1 gallon of paint. A hardware store sells 1-pint cans of paint for $4, 1-quart cans for $7.50, and 1-gallon cans for $28. Which size should Gerald buy? Why?

2. Betty needs 10 cups of apple juice to make her special fruit punch. She already has 2 quarts of apple juice. If the grocery store sells apple juice in gallon, quart, and pint jars, which size should Betty buy? How many?

3. Monique invited 15 people to her summer party. She estimates that each person will drink 3 cups of lemonade. If she already has 2 gallons and 2 quarts of lemonade, should she make more? How much?

4. Javier's fish tank holds 10 gallons of water. To clean the tank, he removed half the water. He is refilling the tank with a quart container. How many times does he need to fill the container with clean water?

5. Estimate how many cups of water you drink each day. If you continue drinking the same amount daily, how many days will it take you to drink 2 gallons of water?

Name ______________________________

HOME CONNECTION: EQUIVALENT MEASURES IN MY REFRIGERATOR

Dear Parent or Guardian:

Your child has been learning about customary units of capacity, such as cups, pints, and gallons. For example, your child has learned that there are 8 pints in 1 gallon, 4 cups in 1 quart, and 2 cups in 1 pint. In this assignment, your child will find some items at home that are measured in customary units of capacity. Then he or she will write the same quantity with an equivalent measure.

Find an item in your refrigerator or kitchen that is measured in the unit. Write the name of the item, the quantity of containers, and the capacity of each container. Then write an equivalent measure.

Example

Item: 4 containers of yogurt, each holding 1 cup

Equivalent measure: 4 cups yogurt = 1 qt yogurt

Cup

Item: ________________________________

Equivalent measure: ________________________________

Pint

Item: ________________________________

Equivalent measure: ________________________________

Quart

Item: ________________________________

Equivalent measure: ________________________________

Gallon

Item: ________________________________

Equivalent measure: ________________________________

Name ______________________________

Measuring Madness

THE FIRST DECISION

Alex and Tonya are preparing for a class party. Decide whether the problem should be solved with an exact measurement or whether it can be solved with an estimated measurement. Circle *exact* or *estimate.*

1. Tonya is making her grandmother's recipe for lime cake. The recipe calls for $3\frac{1}{2}$ cups of lime juice. She is measuring how much juice to put in the mixing bowl.

exact estimate

2. Alex is trying to figure out how much space will be needed for the one-legged jump contest. He is measuring the distance that he can jump on one leg.

exact estimate

3. In one game, students will guess how much a mystery package weighs. Alex wants to measure how much the package weighs beforehand so that he'll know who the winner is.

exact estimate

4. A head-standing contest will be held in part of the room. Tonya is going to borrow a rug for the contestants. She measures the length and width of the approximate area where the rug will go.

exact estimate

5. If the weather is warm enough, the party will end with a water balloon toss. Alex is checking the temperature.

exact estimate

THE SECOND DECISION

Draw a line connecting the measurement and the tool.

If you want to measure the . . .	You could use a . . .
1. height of a giraffe	
2. weight of a pumpkin	
3. capacity of a bag	
4. temperature outside	
5. length of a fish	
6. temperature inside an oven	
7. capacity of a bowl	
8. width of sofa	
9. temperature of a bowl of soup	
10. weight of a flower pot	

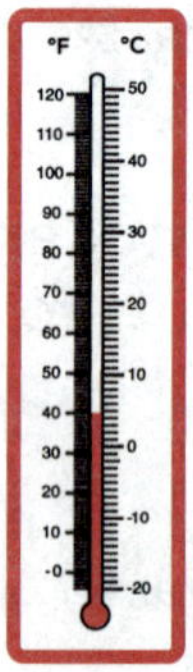

Name ______________________________

YOUR OWN REFERENTS

Use a ruler to find a referent for the unit of length. Then use your referent to estimate the length of the object.

Length	
Customary Unit	Referent
inch	
foot	
yard	

1. A new pencil is about _______ inches long.

2. A door is about _______ feet wide.

3. A third grader is about _______ feet tall.

4. A classroom is about _______ yards long.

5. A hat is about _______ inches tall.

6. A bus is about _______ yards wide.

Use a scale to find a referent for the unit of weight. Then use your referent to estimate the weight of the object.

Weight	
Customary Unit	Referent
ounce	
pound	

7. An orange weighs about _______ ounces.

8. An empty trashcan weighs about _______ pounds.

9. A stapler weighs about _______ ounces.

10. A desk weighs about _______ pounds.

Use a thermometer to find the first three temperatures. Then invent a referent for the fourth temperature.

Temperature	
Unit	Actual Temperature
degree (°) Fahrenheit	mug of hot water: _______ glass of ice water: _______ classroom: _______
	Referent
	100°F day: _______________________

11. A bowl of warm water has a temperature of about _______ Fahrenheit.

12. A cold day in winter has temperature of about _______ Fahrenheit.

Use a measuring tool to find a referent for the unit of capacity. Then use your referent to estimate the capacity of the object.

Capacity	
Customary Unit	Referent
cup	
quart	
gallon	

13. A soup bowl has a capacity of about _______ cups.

14. A bottle of water has a capacity of about _______ cups.

15. A plastic bag has a capacity of about _______ quarts.

16. A bucket has a capacity of about _______ gallons.

HOME CONNECTION: GREAT REFERENTS

Dear Parent or Guardian:

Your child has been learning how to estimate measurements by using referents. A referent is a real-world object that approximates a unit of measure. For example, the length of a boot could be a referent for 1 foot, and you could estimate the length of a room by walking heel to toe from one end of the room to the other. Your child has been working on referents for common units of measure for length, weight, temperature, and capacity. With your help, your child will now find some referents for greater units of measure, including units of time. Encourage your child to be creative!

Find a referent for the unit of measure. Talk with members of your household. Research units in a dictionary or encyclopedia. Think about what would work best to help you estimate measurements.

Customary Unit	Referent
mile	
ton	
minute	
hour	
year	

TOPIC 4

Whole Numbers and Decimals II

Name ______________________________

Grouping Groups

MULTIPLYING TO ADD

Write an addition sentence to solve the problem. Then draw a line connecting the problem to the multiplication sentence that could also be used to solve it.

1. Three students went to the library. Each student checked out 4 books. How many books did the students check out altogether?

2. Ms. Carlisle bought 6 bags of grapefruit. Each bag had 5 grapefruits in it. How many grapefruits did she buy altogether?

3. 

   How many rabbit ears are there?

4. 

   Mr. Smith made a painting of 4 triangles. How many angles did he paint?

5. Jessica rode her bike around a park 5 times. The distance around the park is 7 miles. How many miles did she ride altogether?

6. A cook made 7 pans of muffins. Each pan holds 9 muffins. How many muffins did the cook make?

$5 \times 7 = 35$

$3 \times 4 = 12$

$4 \times 3 = 12$

$7 \times 9 = 63$

$6 \times 5 = 30$

$9 \times 2 = 18$

WHAT IS THE PROBLEM?

Write a word problem for the multiplication sentence.

1. $8 \times 3 = 24$

2. $4 \times 5 = 20$

3. $7 \times 2 = 14$

4. $6 \times 7 = 42$

5. $10 \times 4 = 40$

6. $3 \times 9 = 27$

7. $9 \times 5 = 45$

Name ____

HOME CONNECTION: PLANET GOPI

Dear Parent or Guardian:

Your child has been learning about multiplication by thinking of things that come in groups of equal number. Legs on a dog, for example, come in groups of 4. So, to find the number of legs on 6 dogs, your child has learned to write a multiplication sentence like the following: $6 \times 4 = 24$. In this assignment, your child will read about some imaginary creatures. Then your child will write multiplication sentences to answer questions about the creatures.

Read the descriptions of the creatures from Planet Gopi. Then write and solve a multiplication sentence to answer the question.

On Planet Gopi . . .

A Bumpy Crump has 3 legs and 7 antennae.

A Long-billed Dip has 6 hands, with 1 nose on each hand.

A Zintermoosh grows exactly 10 feet tall.

A Pillyup Perplexer can carry 11 Lumpnuts at one time.

A Wandering Fungle has 4 eyes on both of its heads.

1. If 3 full-grown Zintermooshes are standing on top of one another, how tall are they altogether?

____

____

2. How many Lumpnuts can 5 Pillyup Perplexers carry at one time?

____

____

3. A dance company of Bumpy Crumps has 8 members. How many legs does the company have altogether?

____

____

4. Six Long-billed Dips were smelling the roses. If they were using all of their noses, how many noses were smelling the roses?

____

____

5. Seven Wandering Fungles strode into town, looking for pizza. How many eyes were looking for pizza?

____

____

Name ______________________________

Chunk It!

WHAT'S IT ALL ABOUT?

Solve the problem. Use the picture or information in the problem to help you.

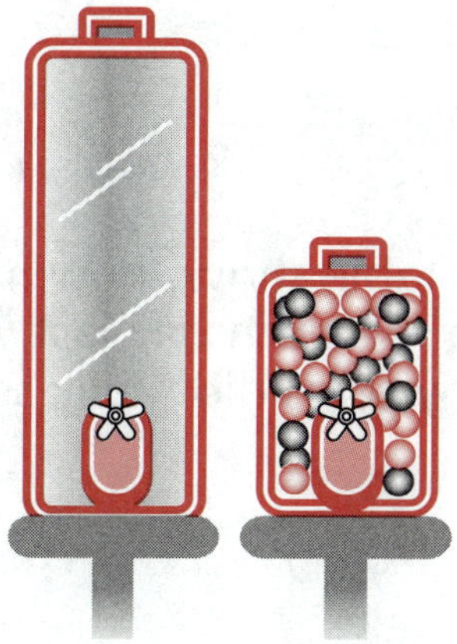

1. Brendan's Bakery has two gum ball machines. Brendan just filled the smaller machine with about 150 gum balls. Approximately how many gum balls will he need to fill the larger machine?

2. Ralph went bowling on Saturday. His scores for the games were 116, 124, 119, 125, 128, and 112. About what was Ralph's total score for all the games together?

3. Cecilia poured close to 40 milliliters of juice into the container. About how many milliliters of juice will the container hold in all?

4. The table shows how many chickens are in each of Lupe's chicken coops. About how many chickens does Lupe have altogether?

Coop	1	2	3	4	5	6
Number of Chickens	22	14	18	23	26	22

5. The car at the right is about 12 feet long. About how long is the plane?

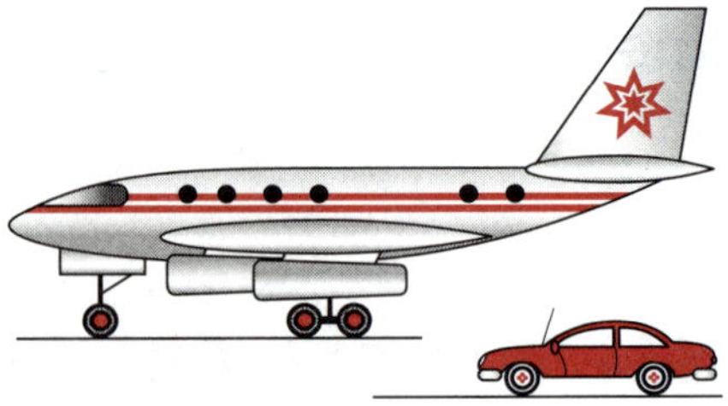

6. The table shows how many coins Malik sold at the coin fair each day last week. Approximately how many coins did Malik sell last week?

Day	Number of Coins Sold
Mon.	29
Tues.	33
Wed.	38
Thurs.	21
Fri.	27
Sat.	35
Sun.	32

7. The ribbons Meg pulled from a box were 11 in., 6 in., 14 in., 8 in., and 12 in. long. She laid the ribbons end to end on the floor. About how long were the ribbons altogether?

8. Kerry is standing next to the school's flagpole. She is about 5 ft tall. About how tall is the flagpole?

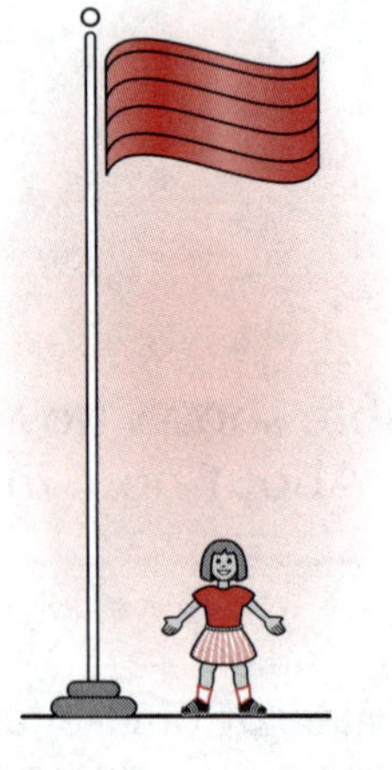

Name ______________________________

HOME CONNECTION: AROUND AND ABOUT

Dear Parent or Guardian:

Your child has been learning how to estimate quantities using either a *referent* or *chunking*. A *referent* is a visual benchmark, such as the number of jelly beans in a small jar, that can be used for estimating another unknown quantity, such as the number of jelly beans in a large jar.

Your child can use *chunking* to estimate the sum of a set of numbers, if the numbers in the set are all close to a benchmark number. For example, if there are 6 numbers in a set and each number is close to 10, your child could multiply 10 and 6 to estimate the sum of the numbers in the set.

Please help your child use either chunking or a referent to solve the problems on the next page.

Solve the problem. Use the picture or information in the problem to help you.

1. The turtle is about 2 feet long. About how long is the alligator?

2. Tim went to several basketball games this year. The school team scored 93, 85, 88, 91, 96, 94, and 82 points at those games. How many points did the team score in all at the games that Tim saw?

3. Emily collects stamps. The table below shows how many stamps are in each of her stamp books. How many stamps does Emily have in all?

Stamp Book	1	2	3	4	5	6	7	8
Number of Stamps	75	84	82	77	84	78	79	81

4. Roger has two jars of marbles. The small jar has about 75 marbles in it. About how many marbles are in the large jar?

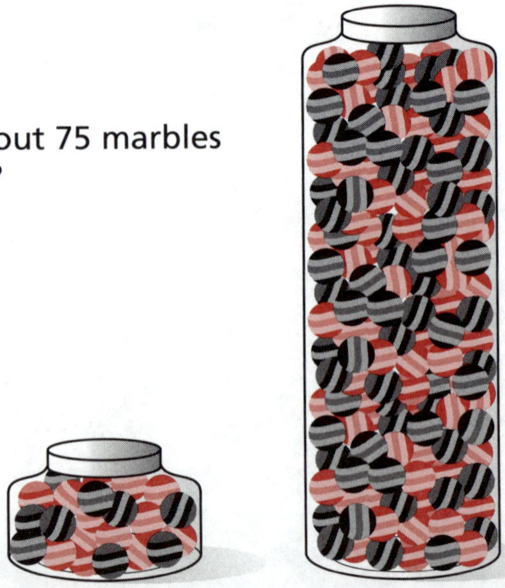

Name ______________________________

Product Development

MY PRODUCT MAT

Name ______________________________

FROM ARRAYS TO NUMBERS

Fill in the blanks to make a number sentence that expresses the array.

1.

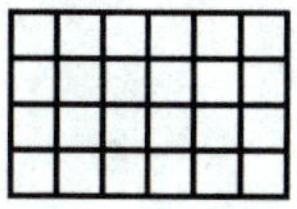

4 • ___ = 24

2.

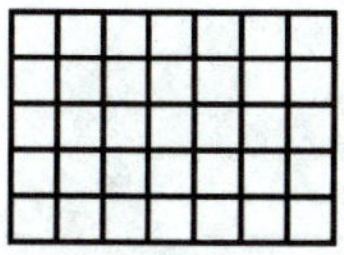

___ • 7 = 35

3.

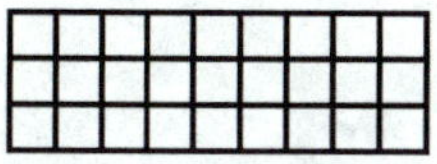

___ • ___ = ___

4.

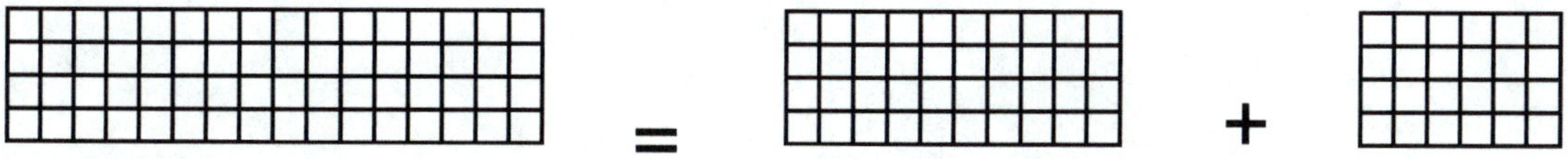

4 • 16 = 4 • 10 + 4 • ___

5.

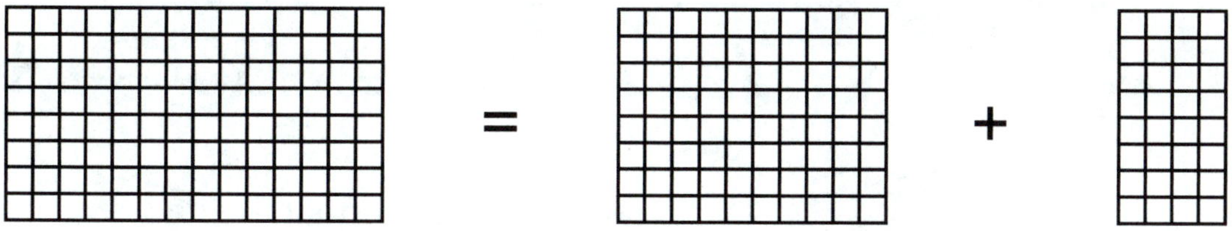

8 • 14 = 8 • ___ + ___ • ___

6.

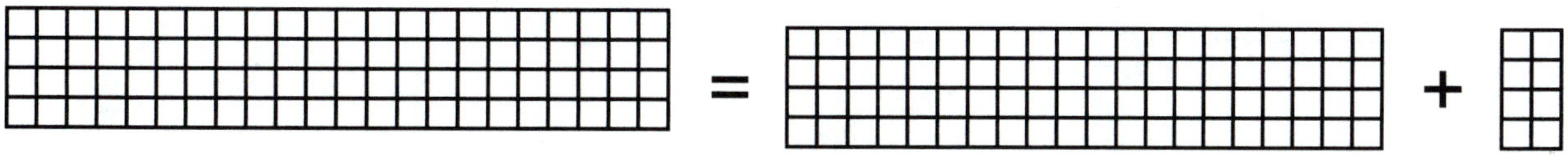

___ • ___ = 4 • 20 + ___ • ___

Fill in the blanks to make the number sentences true.

7. $\underline{6} \cdot \underline{15} = \underline{6} \cdot \underline{10} + \underline{6} \cdot \underline{\quad}$

8. $\underline{19} \cdot \underline{7} = \underline{10} \cdot \underline{\quad} + \underline{\quad} \cdot \underline{7}$

9. $\underline{\quad} \cdot \underline{\quad} = \underline{8} \cdot \underline{20} + \underline{8} \cdot \underline{3}$

10. $\begin{array}{r} 17 \\ \times\ 3 \\ \hline \end{array} = \underline{3} \cdot \underline{10} + \underline{3} \cdot \underline{\quad}$

Fill in the blanks to find the partial products. Then add the partial products to solve the problem.

11. $\begin{array}{r} 68 \\ \times\ 7 \\ \hline \end{array} = \begin{array}{l} \underline{\quad} \cdot \underline{60} = \underline{420} \rightarrow \\ \underline{7} \cdot \underline{8} = \underline{56} \rightarrow \end{array} \begin{array}{r} 420 \\ +\ 56 \\ \hline \end{array}$

These two results are equal.

12. $\begin{array}{r} 55 \\ \times\ 9 \\ \hline \end{array} = \begin{array}{l} \underline{9} \cdot \underline{50} = \underline{\quad} \rightarrow \\ \underline{\quad} \cdot \underline{5} = \underline{\quad} \rightarrow \end{array} \begin{array}{r} \\ + \quad \\ \hline \end{array}$

Name ______________________________

13.

$$\begin{array}{r} 89 \\ \times\ 2 \\ \hline \end{array} = \begin{array}{l} \_\_\_\_ \bullet \_\_\_\_ = \_\_\_\_ \rightarrow \\ \_\_\_\_ \bullet \_\_\_\_ = \_\_\_\_ \rightarrow + \_\_\_\_ \end{array}$$

14.

$$\begin{array}{r} 46 \\ \times\ 4 \\ \hline \end{array} = \begin{array}{l} \_\_\_\_ \bullet \_\_\_\_ = \_\_\_\_ \rightarrow \\ \_\_\_\_ \bullet \_\_\_\_ = \_\_\_\_ \rightarrow + \_\_\_\_ \end{array}$$

15.

$$\begin{array}{r} 33 \\ \times\ 9 \\ \hline \end{array} = \begin{array}{l} \_\_\_\_ \bullet \_\_\_\_ = \_\_\_\_ \rightarrow \\ \_\_\_\_ \bullet \_\_\_\_ = \_\_\_\_ \rightarrow + \_\_\_\_ \end{array}$$

16.

$$\begin{array}{r} 28 \\ \times\ 8 \\ \hline \end{array} = \begin{array}{l} \_\_\_\_ \bullet \_\_\_\_ = \_\_\_\_ \rightarrow \\ \_\_\_\_ \bullet \_\_\_\_ = \_\_\_\_ \rightarrow + \_\_\_\_ \end{array}$$

WHEN TO MULTIPLY

Read each problem. Use what you know about multiplication and using partial products to solve each.

1. Justin has 28 collectible toy cars. Seven of them have doors that open and close. Each one of his cars cost Justin $3. How much did Justin pay for all of his collectible toy cars?

$$\begin{array}{r} 28 \\ \times\ 3 \\ \hline \end{array} \quad = \quad \begin{array}{l} \underline{3} \cdot \underline{20} = \underline{60} \\ \underline{3} \cdot \underline{8} = \underline{24} \end{array} \qquad \begin{array}{r} 60 \\ +\ 24 \\ \hline \$84 \end{array}$$

2. Five buses took the third grade classes on a field trip to the museum. Each bus carried 42 students. How many students took buses to the museum?

3. Every child in Ms. Patrice's class received 3 free books when the bookmobile visited the school. Ms. Patrice has 24 students in her class. How many free books did the students in Ms. Patrice's class receive?

4. In the first week of the gift wrap sale, Kate's class sold 38 rolls of wrapping paper. Each roll costs $5. How much money did Kate's class make?

Name ____

5. Eight students brought cupcakes to the school party. Each one brought a container with 16 cupcakes. How many cupcakes did the students bring to the school party?

6. At the grocery store, Chip bought 4 packages of vanilla creme cookies and 6 packs of oatmeal cookies. There are 38 vanilla creme cookies in each pack and 18 oatmeal cookies in each pack. How many vanilla creme cookies did Chip buy?

7. At the baseball tournament, there were seven games being played at the same time. Each baseball team has nine players on it. How many baseball players were playing in the tournament?

8. Freezy-pops are sold in boxes of eight. This week, Foodmart has Freezy-pops on sale for $3 a box. For the big sale, Foodmart ordered 72 boxes of Freezy-pops. How many individual Freezy-pops did Foodmart order for the sale?

HOME CONNECTION: MY WORD PROBLEMS

Dear Parent or Guardian:

Your child has been learning how to use partial products to solve multiplication problems. Here is an example of how to break down a number, find the partial products, and then add the partial products to solve the problem.

68		$7 \times 60 = 420$	420
$\times$ 7	=	$7 \times 8 = 56$	+ 56
476			476

Your child has been using this strategy to solve word problems. Now he or she is going to write two word problems that require that a 2-digit number be multiplied by a 1-digit number, as in the example above. You can help your child by reading the problems and checking that they meet the requirements. If your child wants to use money amounts, check that they are written as 2-digit amounts, such as $12 or $35.

Write a word problem in each of the boxes. Your word problem should require that a 2-digit number be multiplied by a 1-digit number. Bring your word problems to class for your classmates to solve.

1.

2.

Name ____________________

Teamwork

TEAM CIRCLES

Name ______________________________

SHOW HOW TO DIVIDE

Read each problem. Decide if it can be solved with division, and write *yes* or *no*. If *yes*, write the division sentence and solve it. If *no*, write the kind of number sentence that can be used and solve it. You can draw pictures to help you solve the problems.

1. Katie's mom wants to buy 16 cups of pudding at the store. Each package contains four cups. How many packages of pudding does Katie's mom need to buy?

   Division? Number sentence:

   Picture

2. Mr. Greene's class of thirty students is going on a field trip to the performing arts center. They are riding in five vans. If each van takes the same number of students, how many students will go in each van?

   Division? Number Sentence:

   Picture

3. Joe collects model cars. He has six model cars and a case that holds 24 cars. If each car costs $5, how much money has Joe spent on model cars?

   Division? Number Sentence:

   Picture

4. Jermaine has 24 math problems for homework. He can finish three problems every minute. How many minutes will Jermaine need to finish his homework?

Division? Number Sentence:

Picture:

5. There are thirty-five students in Mrs. Baker's class. Twenty-four of them ride the bus to school. There are only four school buses to carry the students. How many students from Mrs. Baker's class do not ride the bus?

Division? Number Sentence:

Quotient:

6. Mr. Chavez is planting a garden. He wants to plant 42 vegetable plants. He has dug six rows for the plants. If Mr. Chavez places the same number of plants in each row, how many plants will be in each row?

Division? Number Sentence:

Picture:

7. Twenty planes took off at the air show. They flew up into the sky and formed groups of four. How many groups of four did the planes form?

Division? Number Sentence:

Picture:

Name ______________________________

CAN YOU DIVIDE?

1	2	3	4	5
6	7	8	9	10
7 Students	14 Students	21 Students	28 Students	72 Students
35 Students	24 Students	16 Students	18 Students	12 Students
36 Students	40 Students	42 Students	49 Students	8 Students
45 Students	50 Students	54 Students	56 Students	60 Students
15 Students	10 Students	27 Students	32 Students	63 Students

Name ______________________________

HOME CONNECTION: MY DIVISION PROBLEMS

Dear Parent or Guardian:

Your child has been learning how to divide a 2-digit number by a 1-digit number and then using these skills to solve word problems. In this activity, your child will first solve some division problems similar to the ones he or she has been doing in class and then use the same numbers to write word problems. You might have your child read aloud the word problems he or she writes. Doing so can help clarify math concepts and at the same time provide reading practice. You can also help by encouraging your child to use details from around the home in the word problems.

Solve each division sentence. Then, write a word problem for each one on the reverse side of this page.

1. $18 \div 3 =$

2. $24 \div 6 =$

3. $35 \div 7 =$

4. $42 \div 7 =$

1.

2.

3.

4.

Name ______________________________

Multiplication–Division Tango

SHOULD I MULTIPLY OR DIVIDE?

Read each problem, and draw a model to show the problem. Decide which operation (multiplication or division) the model shows, and solve the problem. Then write a number sentence that shows how you solved the problem.

Example: Sixteen pieces of candy are shared equally by 4 students. How many pieces of candy does each student get?

Model:

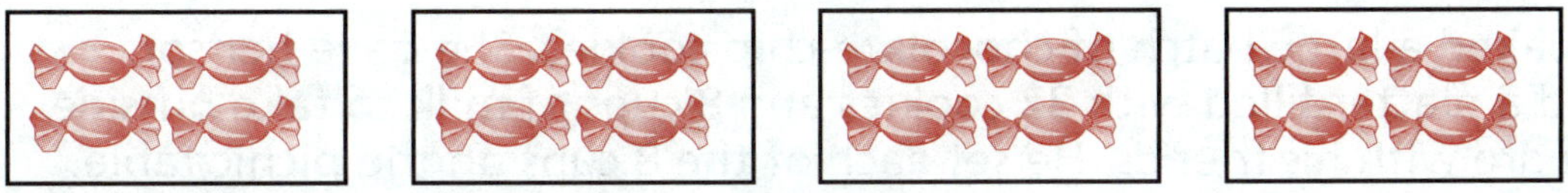

Circle the correct operation. **Multiplication** **Division**

Solution: Each student gets 4 pieces of candy. **Number sentence: 16 ÷ 4 = 4**

---

1. Ivan bought 7 containers of tennis balls. Each container has 3 balls inside. How many tennis balls did Ivan buy?

Model:

Circle the correct operation. **Multiplication** **Division**

Solution: **Number sentence:**

---

2. Linda's father gave her 20 tickets for rides at the carnival. She is going to share them equally with 3 of her friends. How many tickets will each of the 4 people receive?

Model:

Circle the correct operation. **Multiplication** **Division**

Solution: **Number sentence:**

3. Harry bought 5 packs of grape-flavored gum. Each pack contains 8 pieces. How many pieces of gum are in all of the packs?

Model:

Circle the correct operation. **Multiplication** **Division**

Solution: **Number sentence:**

---

4. Julia baked a large batch of chocolate-chip cookies. She gave her son Arnold a platter filled with 32 cookies and 8 cups of milk to take outside and share with his friends. He set each of the 8 cups on the picnic table. How many cookies should he set next to each cup of milk?

Model:

Circle the correct operation. **Multiplication** **Division**

Solution: **Number sentence:**

---

5. Tommy, John, Steve, and Carlton are going to play marbles. Each of the boys reaches into his pocket and grabs a handful of marbles. Each puts his marbles in the center of the table. They count 46 marbles. How many marbles will each boy receive after they divide them evenly? Are there any marbles left over? How many?

Model:

Circle the correct operation. **Multiplication** **Division**

Solution: **Number sentence:**

Name ______________________________

A NUMBER OF PROBLEMS

Read each problem, and use multiplication or division to find the answer. Write a number sentence for each. Draw models if you wish.

Example: Theo found 42 baseball cards in his grandparents' attic. His grandfather told him to split them evenly with his 2 brothers. How many cards will each of them receive?

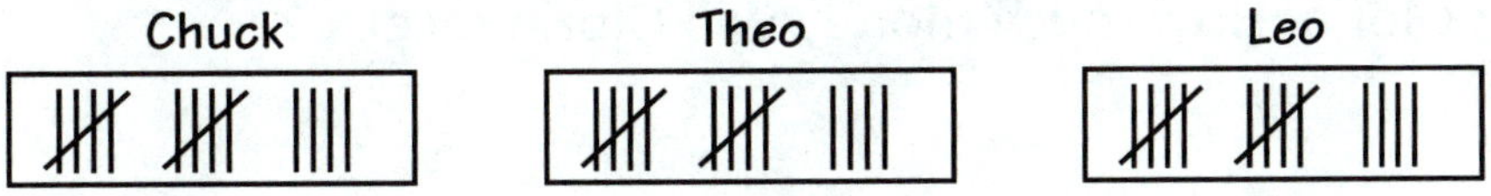

Number Sentence: $42 \div 3 = 14$

1. Linda, Rose, and Alyssa gathered 36 conch shells while snorkeling in the Florida Keys. If they divide the shells evenly, how many will each of the girls get?

Number Sentence: ______________________________

2. Lynn, Anita, and Carol each purchased 5 blouses at the local mall. How many blouses did they buy in all?

Number Sentence: ______________________________

3. Sandy's shell collection contains 4 of each of the following types of shells.

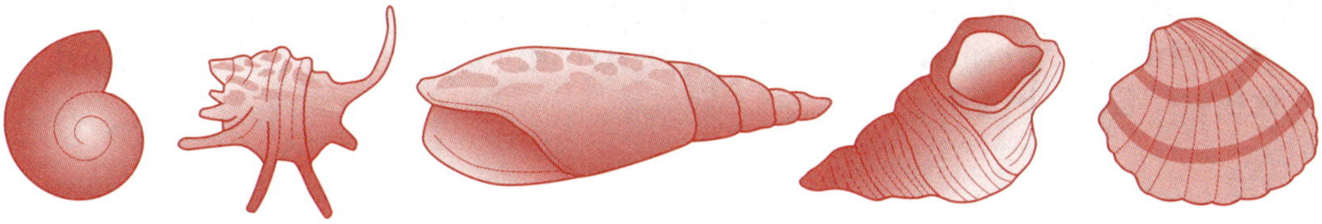

How many shells does Sandy have in all?

Number Sentence: ______________________________

4. Mr. Soriano brought in 72 lollipops for his 12 students. How many lollipops will each of the students receive if he divides them evenly among the students?

Number Sentence: ______________________________

5. Roland found 96 cents in his backyard. He decided to split the money with his sister Gloria. How much money will Gloria receive?

Number Sentence: ______________________________

6. Joshua is baking cookies for 7 of his friends. He would like to give each of them 5 cookies. How many cookies should he bake so that he can give each of them 5 cookies?

Number Sentence: ______________________________

7. Liza likes to read fiction books. Each day during her 10-day vacation, she read 3 books. How many books did she read while she was on vacation?

Number Sentence: ______________________________

8. Abe, Josh, and Ben found a sack filled with 41 gold coins. They decided to divide them evenly among the 3 of them, and if any remained, they would give the extra coins to Josh's sister Anne. How many coins should Anne receive? Explain why.

Number Sentence: ______________________________

Name ______________________________

HOME CONNECTION: MULTIPLY OR DIVIDE?

Dear Parent or Guardian:

Your child has been reading word problems, drawing models to represent the problems, choosing whether to use multiplication or division to solve the problems, and writing number sentences to solve the problems.

For this activity, your child will write three word problems that involve members of the household or household items. Help your child with drawing the models to show the problems, choosing the operations, and finding the solutions. Your child will record his or her word problems and models on the reverse side of this page.

- **Write three word problems that involve someone in your home or items in your home.**
- **Follow the example problem at the top of the page.**
- **Be sure to circle the correct operation and write a number sentence for each word problem.**

Multiplication or Division

Example: Twelve notebooks are shared equally by 3 students.
How many notebooks does each student have?

Model:

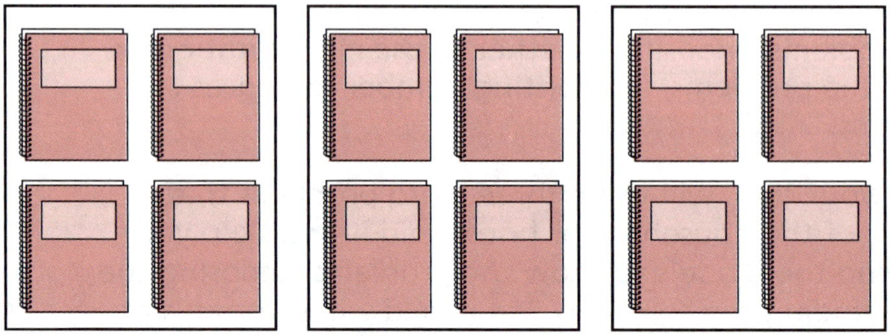

Circle the correct operation. **Multiplication** **Division**

Solution: Each student has 4 notebooks. Number sentence: $12 \div 3 = 4$

1.

2.

3.

Name ______________________________

"T" It Up!

THE POINT OF T-CHARTS

1. Brett went to Busch Gardens. He bought food to feed the ducks. For 1 quarter, he received 10 pellets. For 2 quarters, he received 20 pellets. If the pattern continues, how many pellets will he get if he pays 4 quarters? 10 quarters? 50 quarters? One hundred quarters?

Number of Quarters	Number of Pellets
1	10
2	20
3	30
4	
5	
•	•
•	•
10	
50	
100	
n	?

2. At the domino-pattern competition, players for Team Dominotor had 2 dominoes in Row 1 of their pattern. Row 2 had 4 dominoes. Row 3 had 6 dominoes. How many dominoes were in Row 4? Row 10? Row 20? Row 50?

Row Number	Number of Dominoes
1	2
2	4
3	6
4	
5	
•	•
•	•
10	
20	
50	
n	?

T-CHARTS, T-CHARTS, T-CHARTS!

T-Chart 1 

Number of Triangles	Number of Line Segments
1	3
2	6
3	9
11	

T-Chart 2 

Number of Squares	Number of Line Segments
1	4
2	

T-Chart 3 

Number of Hands	Number of Fingers
1	5
2	10
3	15
4	
5	
6	
•	•
•	•
•	•
20	
50	
100	

Workspace

Name ______________________________

T-CHART SOLUTIONS

1. Laurie wants to save her allowance so she can buy a $275.00 stereo system for her room. Each week, after completing her chores, Laurie receives an allowance of 25 dollars. For how many weeks will Laurie have to save her allowance to buy the stereo system?

Number of Weeks	Total Money Saved
1	$25.00
2	
3	
4	
5	

Rule: ______________

2. On Day 2 of Jack Custoh's fishing venture, his crew caught 40 fish. On Day 4, they caught 80 fish, and on Day 6, they caught 120 fish. If the pattern continues, how many fish will be caught on Day 20? Day 50? Day 100?

Day Number	Number of Fish Caught
2	40
4	80
6	120
8	
10	
•	•
•	•
•	•
20	
50	
100	

Rule: ______________

3. Leon has a dog-walking business called "Your Dog's Best Friend." Every day, he picks up a dog and walks it around the neighborhood. The 30-minute walk earns him $8.00 per day. He walks a total of 7 dogs each week. How many walks will he have taken after 11 weeks?

Number of Weeks	Walks Taken
1	7

Rule: ______________

4. For how many minutes will Leon have walked after 9 weeks if he continues walking for 210 minutes per week?

Week	Minutes Walked
1	210
2	

Rule: ______________

Name ______________________________

HOME CONNECTION: INPUT-OUTPUT

Dear Parent or Guardian:

Your child has been introduced to the concept of an input-output rule, meaning that, using a certain number as an input, a rule is applied to that number, and a certain number becomes the output. For example, if the rule is $n + 2$, and the input number is 3, then the output number would be $3 + 2$, or 5. Your child has learned to express the application of these rules in T-charts. Here is an example of a T-chart that shows the results of input and output if the rule is $n \times 2$.

Rule: $n \times 2$

Input	Output
2	4
3	6
4	8

For this activity, help your child to come up with a rule for each T-chart on the reverse side of this page. Also help your child to write the rule for each T-chart correctly.

- **Write a rule for each T-chart, and show how to fill out each T-chart, according to its rule.**

T-Charts in the Home

T-Chart 1

Input	Output
n	?

Rule: ____________________

T-Chart 2

Input	Output
n	?

Rule: ____________________

T-Chart 3

Input	Output
n	?

Rule: ____________________

T-Chart 4

Input	Output
n	?

Rule: ____________________

Name ____

A Size Factor

GOLD BARS

Cut out each gold bar.

2 cm	2 cm	2 cm	2 cm	2 cm	2 cm	2 cm
2 cm	2 cm	2 cm	2 cm	2 cm	2 cm	2 cm

3 cm	3 cm	3 cm	3 cm	3 cm
3 cm	3 cm	3 cm	3 cm	3 cm

4 cm	4 cm	4 cm
4 cm	4 cm	4 cm

5 cm	5 cm	5 cm
5 cm	5 cm	5 cm

6 cm	6 cm
6 cm	6 cm

7 cm	7 cm
7 cm	7 cm

8 cm
8 cm

Name ______________________________

STEEL BOXES

Pack each size of gold bar in the steel box. Use only one size at a time. Which size bars could completely fill the box? Remember to pack the box the long way and the wide way. Write *yes* or *no* to complete the table on page 171.

Steel Box 1

Steel Box 2

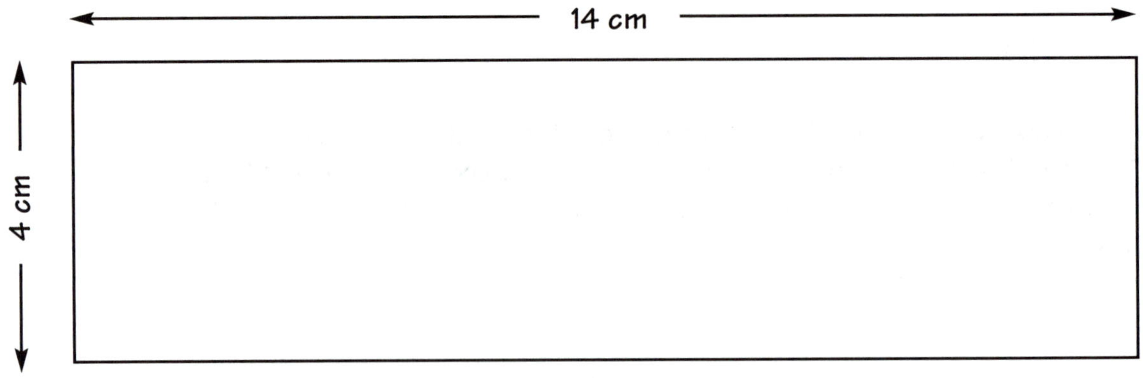

Steel Box 3

Name ______________________________

GOLD BARS IN STEEL BOXES

Could the gold bars completely fill the box? Write *yes* or *no* to complete the table.

Steel Box 1

Packing Direction	Size of Bars						
	2 cm	3 cm	4 cm	5 cm	6 cm	7 cm	8 cm
The Long Way 18 cm							
The Wide Way 15 cm							

Steel Box 2

Packing Direction	Size of Bars						
	2 cm	3 cm	4 cm	5 cm	6 cm	7 cm	8 cm
The Long Way 14 cm							
The Wide Way 4 cm							

Steel Box 3

Packing Direction	Size of Bars						
	2 cm	3 cm	4 cm	5 cm	6 cm	7 cm	8 cm
The Long Way 16 cm							
The Wide Way 10 cm							

A BANKER COUNTS

Write the measurement of each way a gold bar will completely fill a steel box. Write the measurements in order from shortest to longest. The first problem is done for you as an example.

1. 2 cm bar: 4 cm, 10 cm, 14 cm, 16 cm, 18 cm
2. 3 cm bar: ______________________________
3. 4 cm bar: ______________________________
4. 5 cm bar: ______________________________
5. 6 cm bar: ______________________________
6. 7 cm bar: ______________________________
7. 8 cm bar: ______________________________
8. What do you notice about the length of a bar and the measurements of the ways it will fit in a box?

Name ______________________________

HUNDRED TABLE

1	2	3	4	5	6	7	8	9	10
11	12	13	14	15	16	17	18	19	20
21	22	23	24	25	26	27	28	29	30
31	32	33	34	35	36	37	38	39	40
41	42	43	44	45	46	47	48	49	50
51	52	53	54	55	56	57	58	59	60
61	62	63	64	65	66	67	68	69	70
71	72	73	74	75	76	77	78	79	80
81	82	83	84	85	86	87	88	89	90
91	92	93	94	95	96	97	98	99	100

MULTIPLYING MULTIPLES

Complete the multiplication sentences to find the first five multiples of the number.

1. Multiples of 2

$0 \times 2 = 0$, $1 \times 2 =$ ____, $2 \times 2 =$ ____, $3 \times 2 =$ ____, ____ $\times 2 = 8$

2. Multiples of 5

$0 \times 5 =$ ____, $1 \times 5 =$ ____, ____ $\times 5 =$ ____, ____ $\times 5 =$ ____, ____ $\times 5 =$ ____

3. Multiples of 3

____ $\times 3 =$ ____, ____ $\times 3 =$ ____, ____ $\times 3 =$ ____, ____ $\times 3 =$ ____, ____ $\times 3 =$ ____

4. Multiples of 8

____ $\times 8 =$ ____, $1 \times 8 =$ ____, ____ $\times 8 =$ ____, ____ $\times 8 =$ ____, ____ $\times 8 =$ ____

5. Multiples of 6

____ $\times 6 =$ ____, ____ $\times 6 =$ ____, ____ $\times 6 =$ ____, ____ $\times 6 =$ ____, ____ $\times 6 =$ ____

Write the missing multiples to complete the sequence.

6. Multiples of 7

0, 7, ____, 21, ____, 35, 42, ____, 56

7. Multiples of 4

____, ____, 8, 12, ____, ____, 24, 28, ____, 36

8. Multiples of 10

____, ____, ____, 30, 40, ____, ____, ____, ____, ____, 100

9. Multiples of 25

____, ____, 50, ____, ____, ____, 150

10. Multiples of 100

____, 100, ____, ____, ____, 500

Name ______________________________

FACTORING FACTORS

Complete the multiplication sentences to answer the question.

1. What are the factors of 4?

1 × ____ = 4, ____ × 2 = 4

So, 1, ____, and ____ are factors of 4.

2. What are the factors of 7?

____ × 7 = 7

So, ____ and 7 are factors of 7.

3. What are the factors of 15?

1 × ____ = 15, ____ × 5 = 15

So, 1, ____ , 5, and ____ are factors of 15.

4. What are the factors of 24?

1 × ____ = 24, 2 × ____ = 24, ____ × 8 = 24, 4 × ____ = 24

So, 1, ____, ____, 4, ____, ____, ____, and ____ are factors of 24.

5. What are the factors of 100?

____ × 100 = 100, 2 × ____ = 100, ____ × 25 = 100, 5 × ____ = 100, 10 × ____ = 100

So, ____ , 2, ____, 5, 10, ____, ____, ____, and 100 are factors of 100.

Write all the factors of the number.

6. 9 ______________________________

7. 6 ______________________________

8. 18 ______________________________

9. 30 ______________________________

Answer.

10. Which number has the fewest factors? ____

11. Which number has the most factors? ____

MULTIPLES AND FACTORS AT WORK AND PLAY

Solve.

1. A gardener is laying a row of bricks along his fern bed. Each brick is 8 in. long. The fern bed is 72 in. long. Will he need to cut a brick? Explain.

2. Ms. Peterson is trying to decide which size tile to buy to replace her bathroom floor. The bathroom is 60 in. long and 48 in. wide. Ms. Peterson doesn't want to have to cut any tiles. Which size(s) could she buy? Explain.

Bathroom Tiles	
6 in. x 6 in.	10 in. x 10 in.
8 in. x 8 in.	11 in. x 11 in.
9 in. x 9 in.	12 in. x 12 in.

3. A quiltmaker is going to make a quilt that is 56 in. long and 35 in. wide. She'll make the quilt by sewing squares of cloth together. What size squares could she use? Show your answer by drawing squares in the diagram.

Quilt

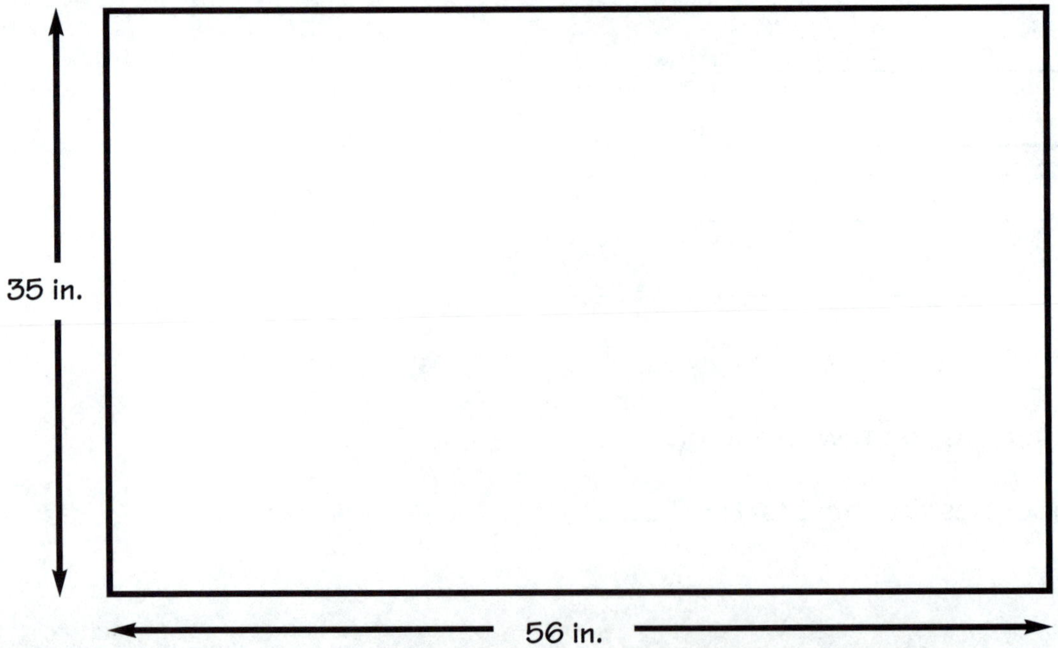

Name ______________________________

HOME CONNECTION: BOOKSHELVES AND BOXES

Dear Parent or Guardian:

Your child has been learning how to find multiples and factors. A multiple is the product of a given number and another number. For example, 12 is a multiple of 6 because $2 \times 6 = 12$. A factor is a number that, when multiplied by another number, gives a certain product. For example, 5 is a factor of 20 because $4 \times 5 = 20$. In the following assignment, your child will measure the lengths of two bookshelves to the nearest inch and find all of the factors for the lengths. Then your child will draw a box with special dimensions: the length and the width will be multiples of only two numbers each.

Measure the length of two different bookshelves to the nearest inch. Write all of the factors of the two lengths.

Bookshelf 1

Length: ____________________

Factors: ____________________

Bookshelf 2

Length: ____________________

Factors: ____________________

Draw a rectangular box. Make the length so that it is a multiple of only two numbers. Make the width so that it is a multiple of only two numbers. Label the length and width.

TOPIC 5

Geomeasure II

Name ____________________

Time Flies

CLOCK FACE

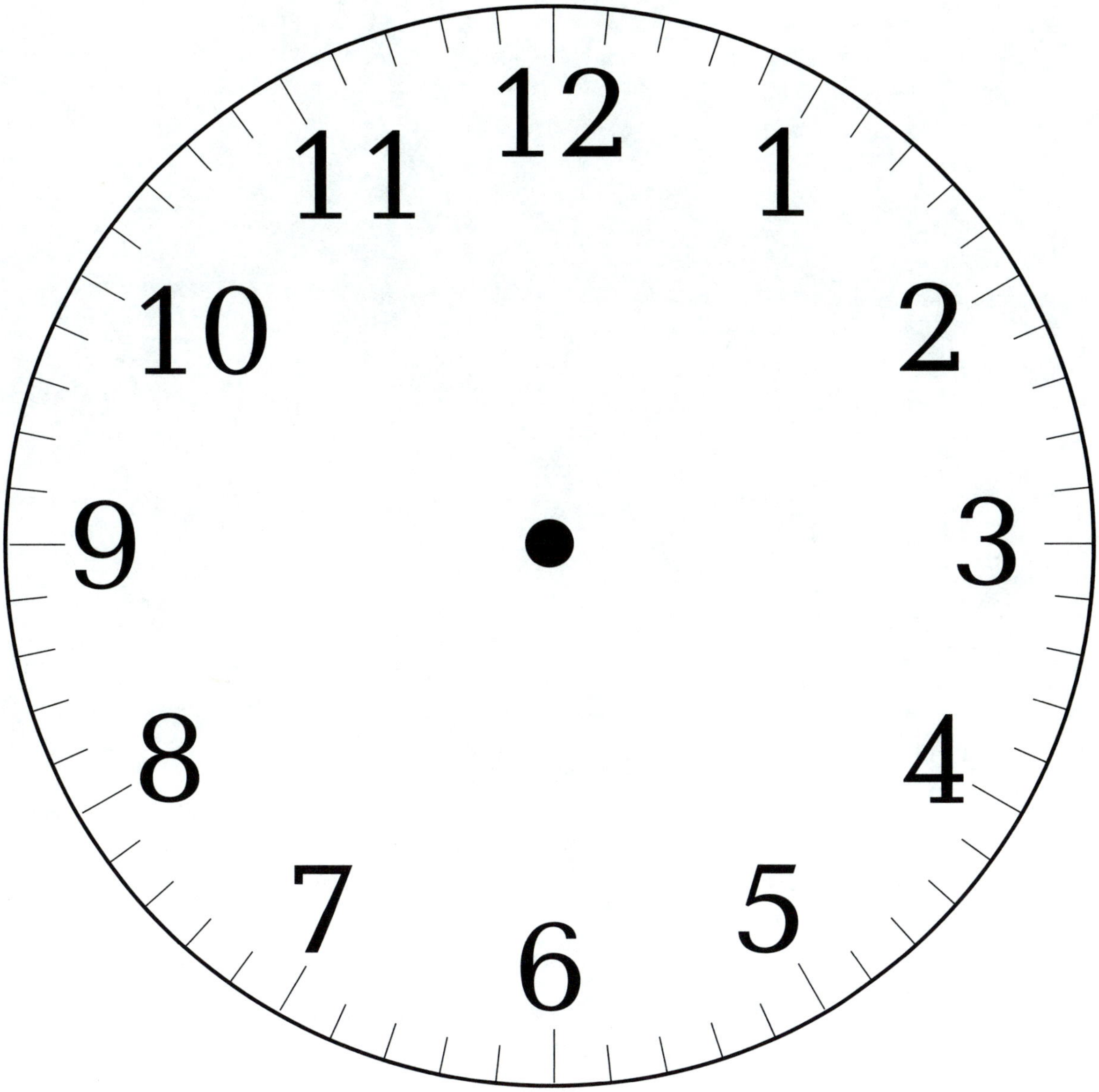

Name ______________________________

FIND THE TIME

Use the clock face, without hands, to solve the problems.

1. Sonia took the bus from Cooperstown to Stoneville. The bus left Cooperstown at 12:25 P.M. and arrived in Stoneville at 3:20 P.M. For how long did Sonia ride the bus?

2. Mark sat down to practice piano at 2:00. He practiced for an hour and a half. At what time did Mark stop practicing?

3. Selma finished gluing her model ship together at 1:05. She left the ship to dry for 45 minutes and then placed the ship on a shelf. At what time did Selma place the ship on the shelf?

4. Paul took the 4:10 train out of Flowers Station and arrived at the Marine Terminal at 5:20. How much time did the train trip take?

5. Sara and Jon began their chess game at 10:00 A.M. Sara won the game at 12:25 P.M. For how much time were Sara and Jon playing chess?

WHERE DID THE TIME GO?

Solve each problem. Use a clock face for help if you wish.

1. Vida and Sam began to work on their science project at 1:15. They worked for 1 hour 15 minutes. They stopped to have lunch and began work on their project again at 2:45. They worked for 2 hours 10 minutes, when they stopped for the day. At what time did they stop?

2. Anita began hockey practice at 9:30 and practiced for 1 hour 10 minutes. Next, she spent 25 minutes taking her uniform to be cleaned and 20 minutes to walk back home. Did Anita arrive at home in time for her 11:30 flute lesson?

3. Jim woke up at 5:30 in the morning. He exercised for 45 minutes. He spent 45 minutes showering, dressing, and eating breakfast. Jim then studied for 1 hour. Then he left the house and walked for 30 minutes to arrive at school. At what time did Jim arrive at school?

4. Lisa left home on Saturday at 11:45 in the morning to run some errands. She returned home in 55 minutes. She spent 1 hour having lunch and then read for 45 minutes. At what time did Lisa stop reading?

5. Rick went to a movie that began at 2:30. The movie ran for 90 minutes. Rick's walk home took 40 minutes. At what time did Rick reach his home?

Name ______________________________

HOME CONNECTION: WHO HAS THE TIME?

Dear Parent or Guardian:

Your child has been learning about elapsed time. Specifically, your child has been learning to use a beginning time and an ending time to find out how much time an event or an activity took. Your child has also been learning to use a beginning time and a span of time to find an ending time.

Help your child to read through the directions. Then provide your child assistance, if necessary, in completing the table on the reverse side of this page. Tell your child that the process can be repeated for other activities for more practice in finding elapsed time.

- **Write the beginning time for the activity in the Beginning Time column of the table. When the activity is finished, write the ending time in the Ending Time column.**
- **Find the elapsed time for the activity, and record it in the Elapsed Time column.**

Time Table

Activity	Beginning Time	Ending Time	Elapsed Time
Doing homework			
Cleaning the room			
Eating dinner			

Name ____________________

Which End's Up?

PENTOMINOES

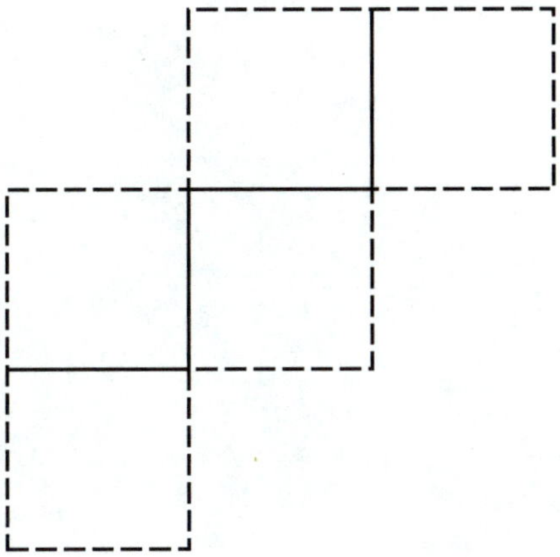

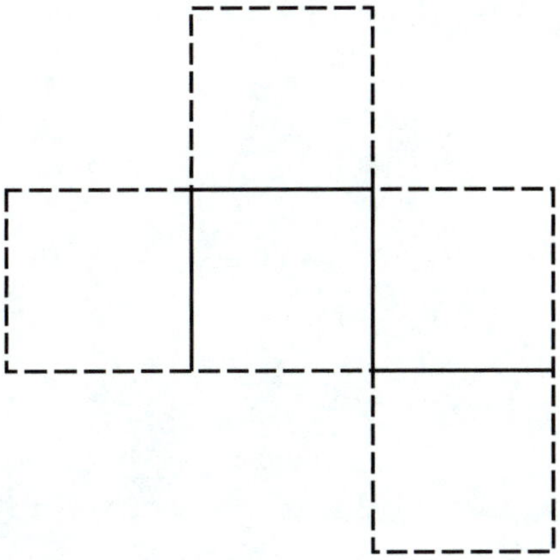

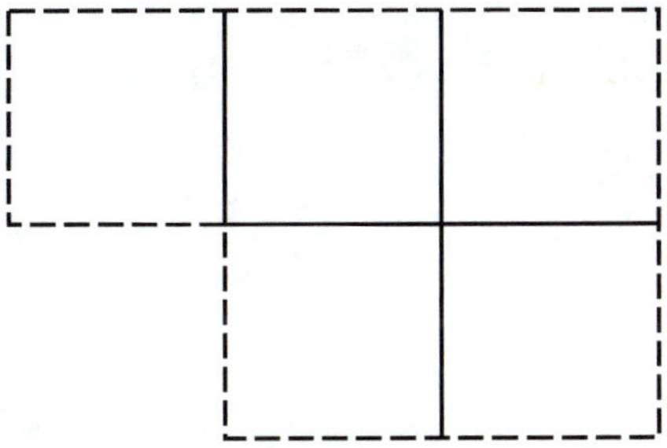

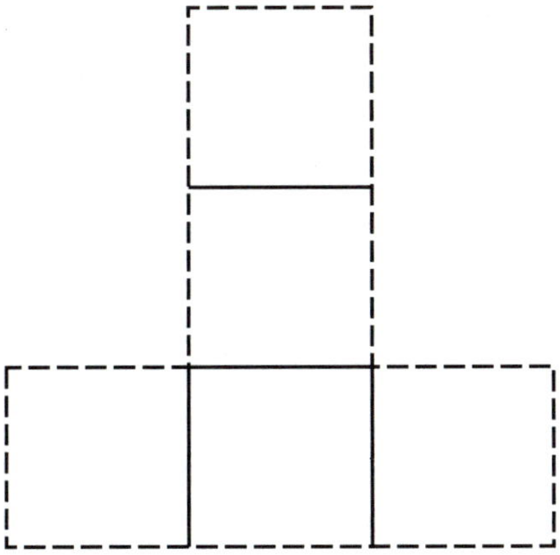

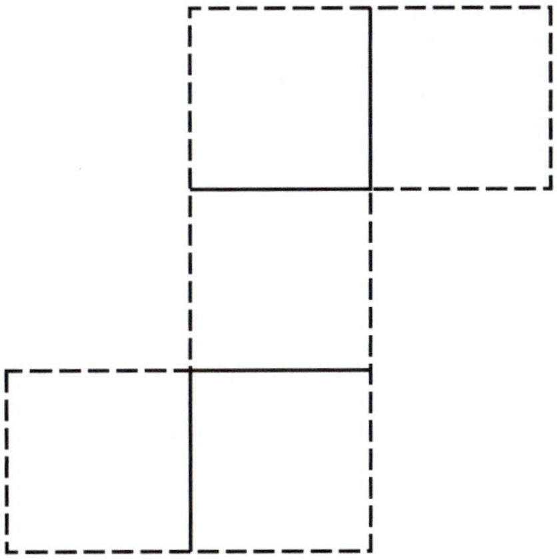

Name ______________________________

THE WORLD'S FLIPPING!

Label each as a flip (reflection), slide (translation), or turn (rotation). If it is a turn, is it a quarter turn, a half turn, or a three-quarter turn?

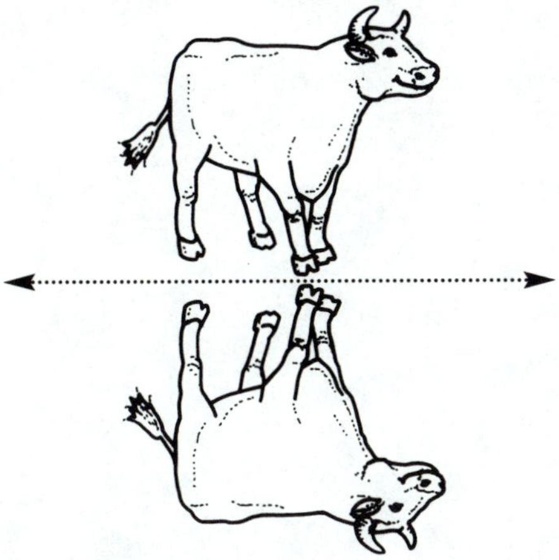

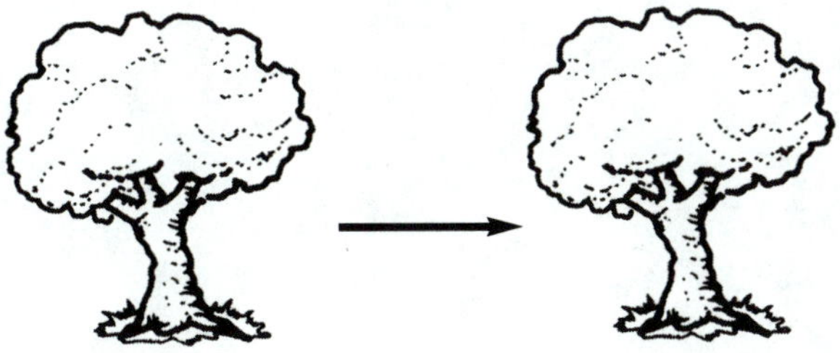

1. ______________________

2. ______________________

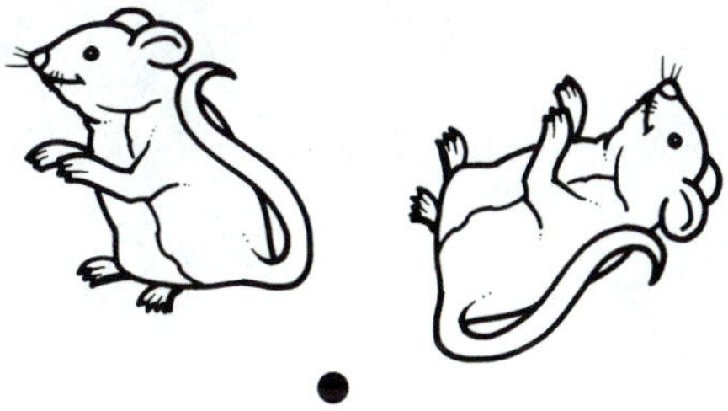

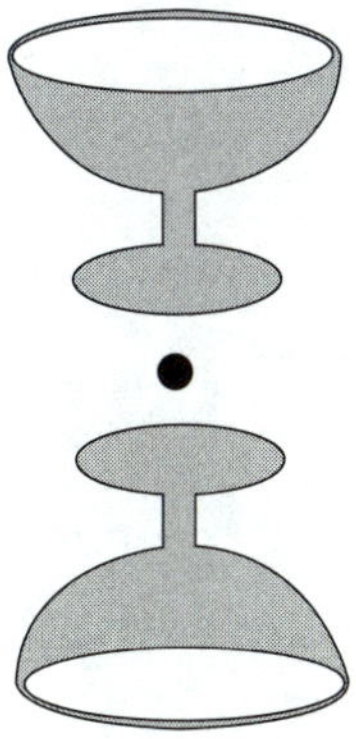

3. ______________________

4. ______________________turn

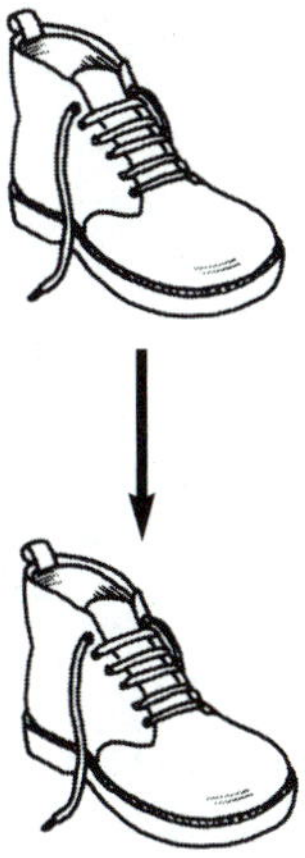

5. ______________________

6. ______________________

Name ______________________________

HOME CONNECTION: TRANSFORMING PENTOMINOES

Dear Parent or Guardian:

Your child has been learning about transformations of figures. Transformations include slides (or translations), turns (or rotations), and flips (or reflections). There are various types of each kind of transformation. An example of each kind of transformation is shown below; the red figure shows the new figure after the transformation.

Slide

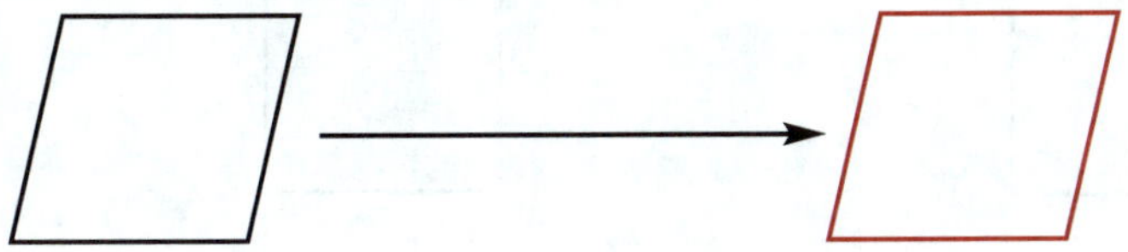

$\frac{1}{4}$ clockwise turn (or 90° clockwise turn)

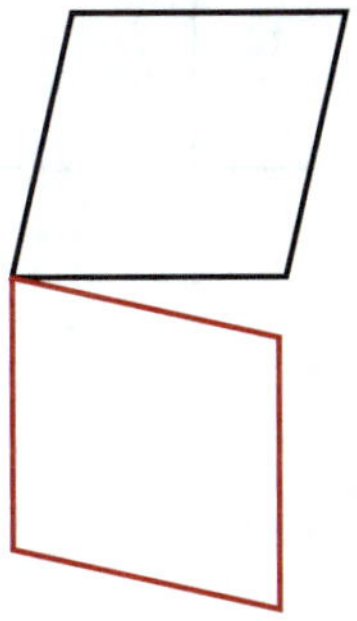

Flip

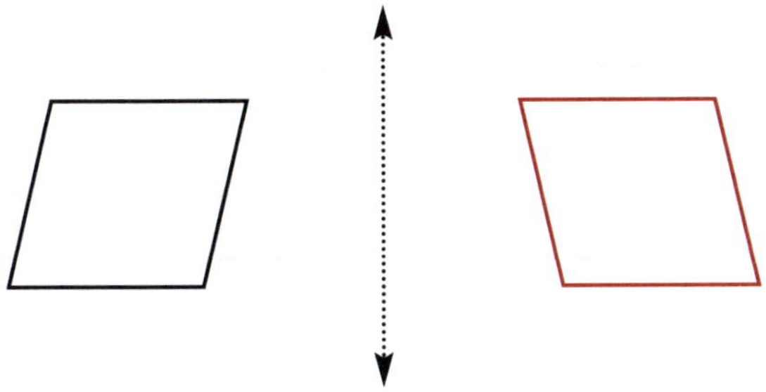

Please help your child with the transformations on the next page.

Cut out the pentominoes on this page. Trace each shape on a sheet of grid paper. Then use the cutouts to perform and trace the following transformations for each pentomino.

1. Slide to the left

2. 180° counterclockwise turn

3. $\frac{3}{4}$ clockwise turn

4. Flip

Name ______________________________

Looks Like Twins

LOOKS LIKE?

Decide if the two figures in a pair are congruent, similar, or neither. Write *C* (for congruent), *S* (for similar), or *N* (for neither).

1. 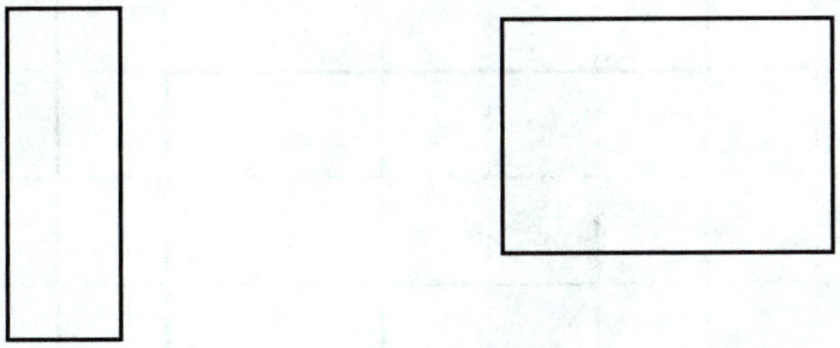 ____

2.  ____

3.  ____

4. 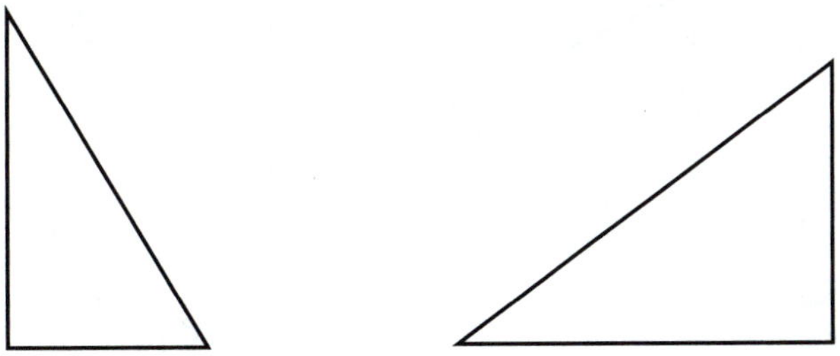 ____

5. 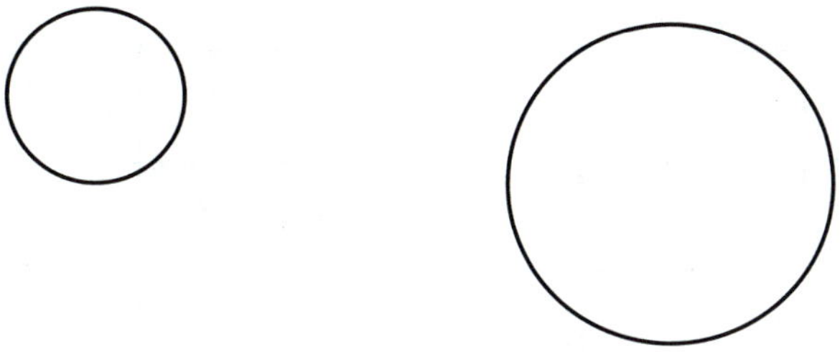 ____

COPYCAT

On grid paper, draw figures that are congruent to the figures below.

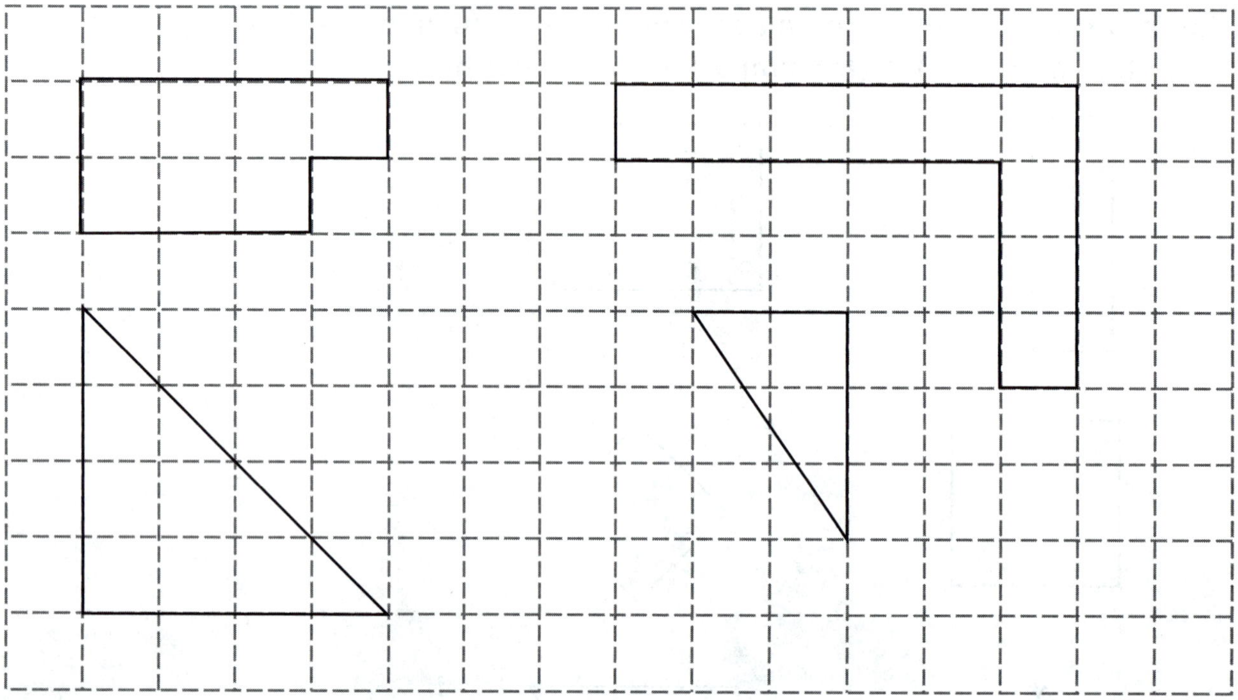

On grid paper, draw figures that are similar to the figures below. Double the length of each side of the figure.

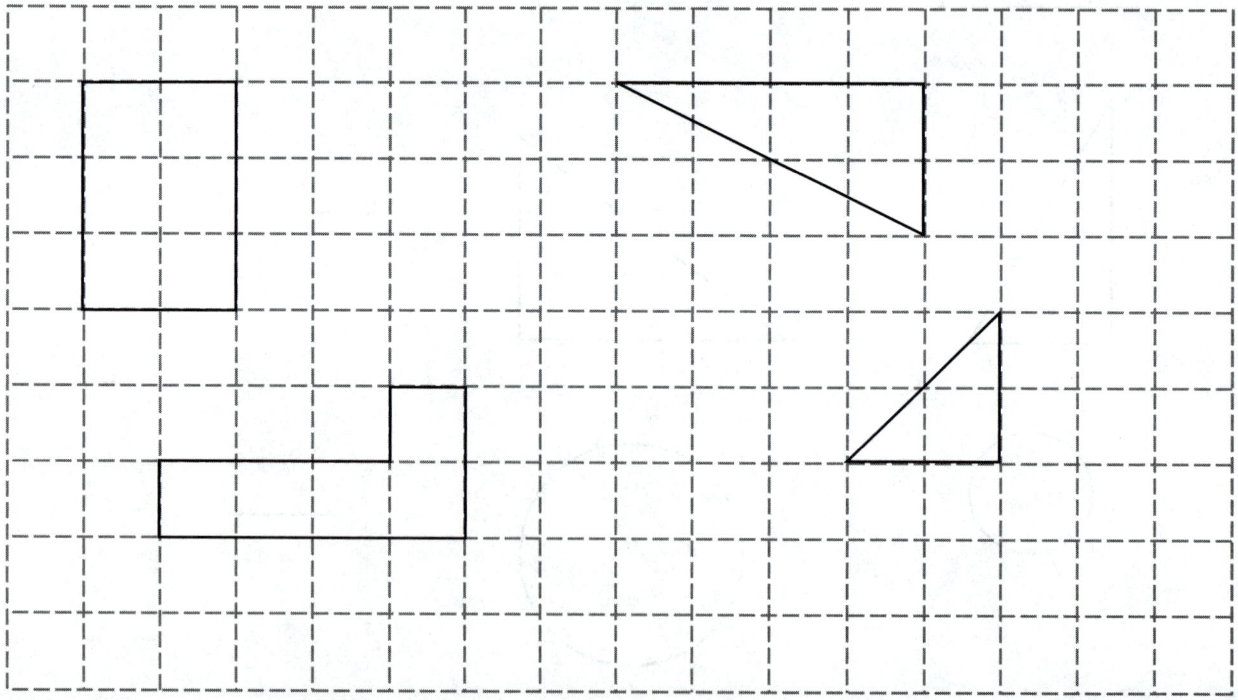

Name ____

HOME CONNECTION: SHAPE AND SIZE

Dear Parent or Guardian:

Your child has been learning about similarity and congruence of figures. Figures are *similar* if they have the exact same shape; they are *congruent* if they have the exact same shape and size. On the other side of this page, your child should list pairs or groups of items at home that are similar, and pairs or groups of items at home that are congruent.

List items in your home that are congruent, and items that are similar.

Congruent Items

Similar Items

Name ____________________

Point to Point

THE BIG DIPPER IN THE SKY

Draw a star at each point named by your teacher. Draw line segments connecting the points to see one of the most famous constellations of the Northern Hemisphere, the Big Dipper. Native Americans include more stars in the constellation and call it the Great Bear.

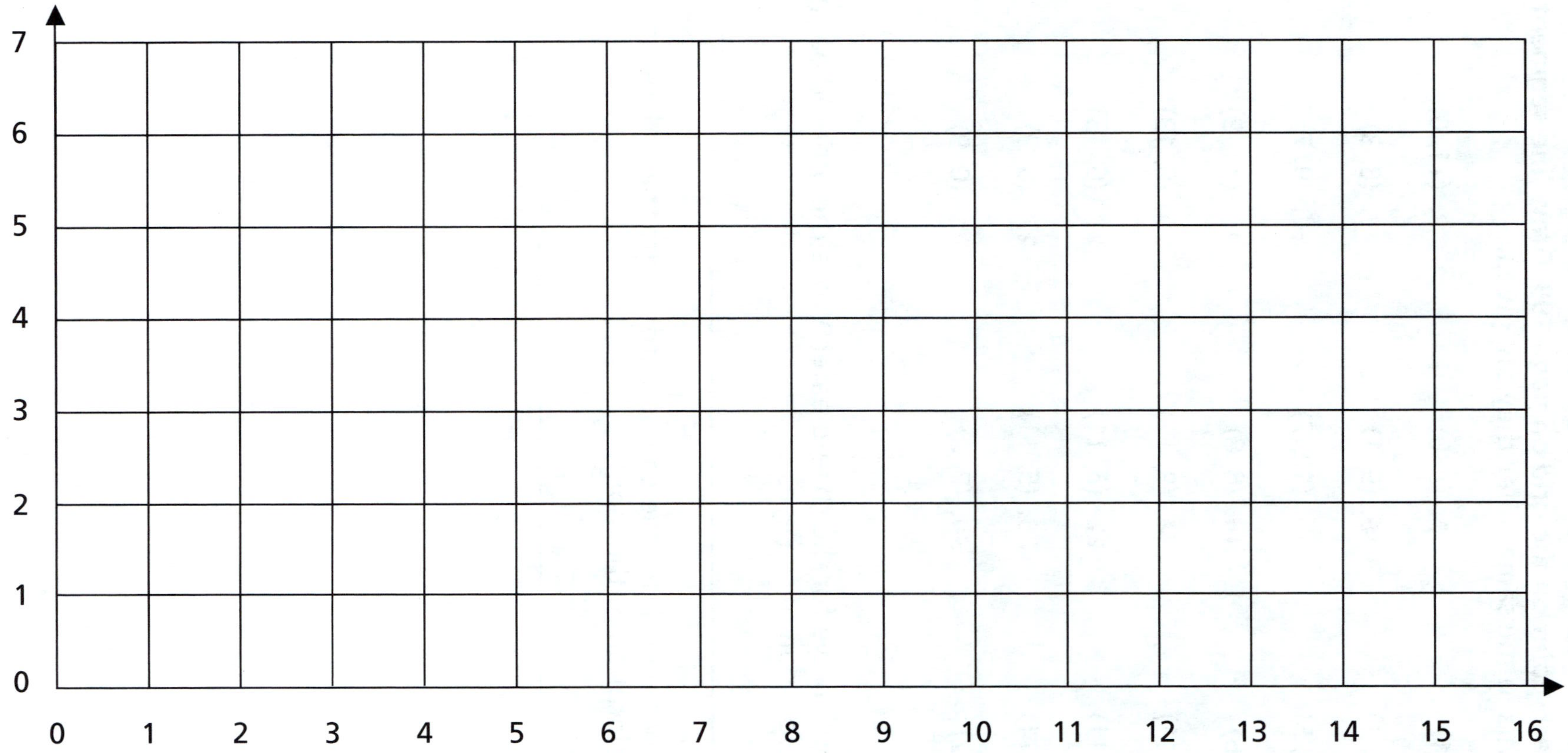

WHERE IS THE CHEESE?

Draw each point on the grid on page 199. Draw line segments connecting the points in the same order they are given.

1. (1, 1)	**2.** (3, 0)	**3.** (11, 0)	**4.** (11, 2)
5. (10, 1)	**6.** (9, 1)	**7.** (8, 3)	**8.** (8, 5)
9. (10, 5)	**10.** (10, 7)	**11.** (9, 7)	**12.** (9, 6)
13. (8, 6)	**14.** (8, 8)	**15.** (11, 9)	**16.** (11, 10)
17. (8, 11)	**18.** (9, 11)	**19.** (9, 13)	**20.** (7, 13)
21. (7, 11)	**22.** (6, 11)	**23.** (6, 13)	**24.** (4, 13)
25. (4, 11)	**26.** (5, 11)	**27.** (5, 9)	**28.** (3, 7)
29. (2, 2)	**30.** (2, 8)	**31.** (0, 9)	**32.** (1, 7)

Solve.

33. Draw an eye for the cheese-eater. Write the ordered pair(s) that show the location of the eye.

____

34. Draw a mouth for the cheese-eater. Write the ordered pair(s) that show the location of the mouth.

____

Name ______________________________

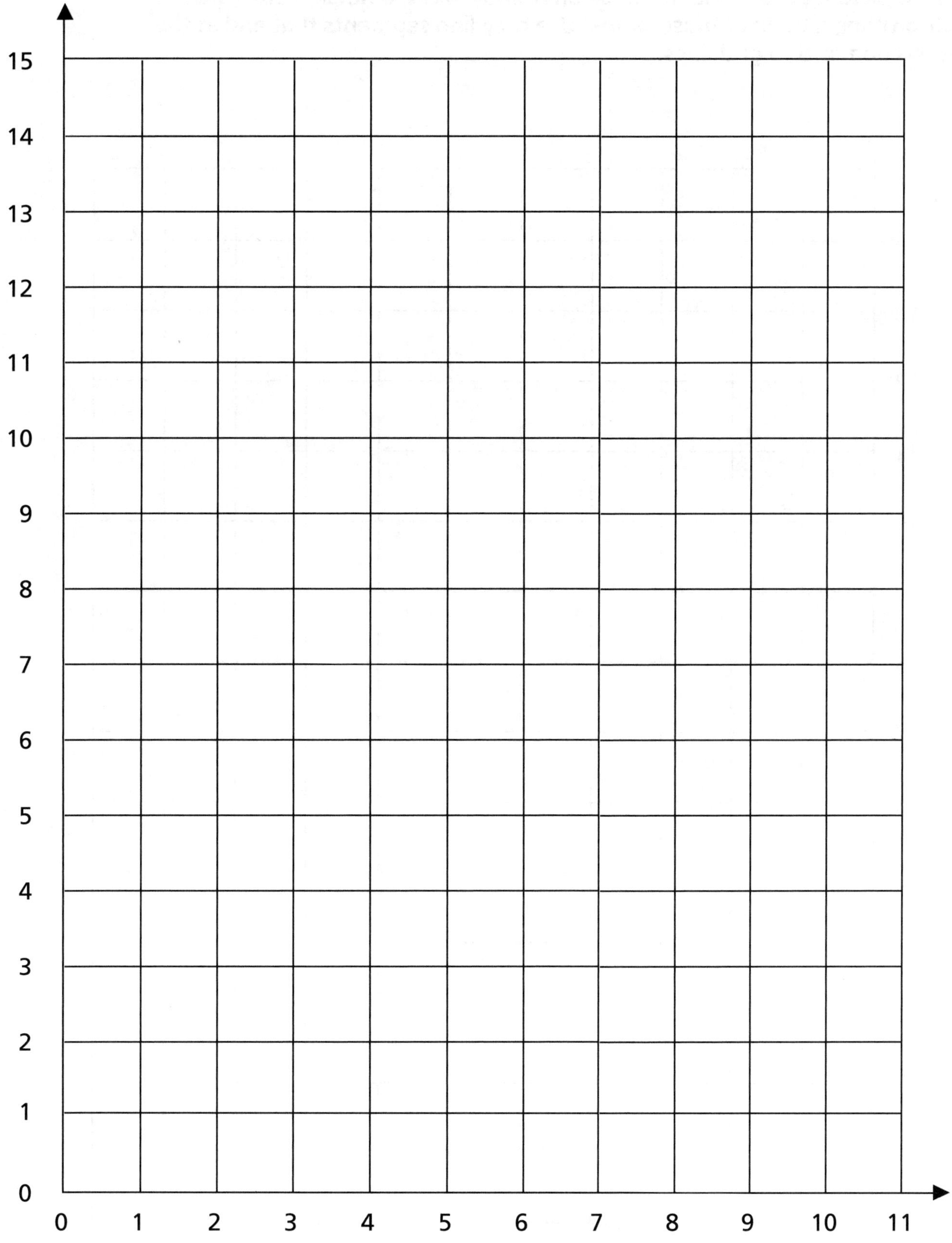

A COORDINATED PICTURE

Draw a picture on the grid. It can be anything—a cat, a horse, your sister, your brother, a bowl of mushrooms! Use only line segments that end at the intersection of two grid lines.

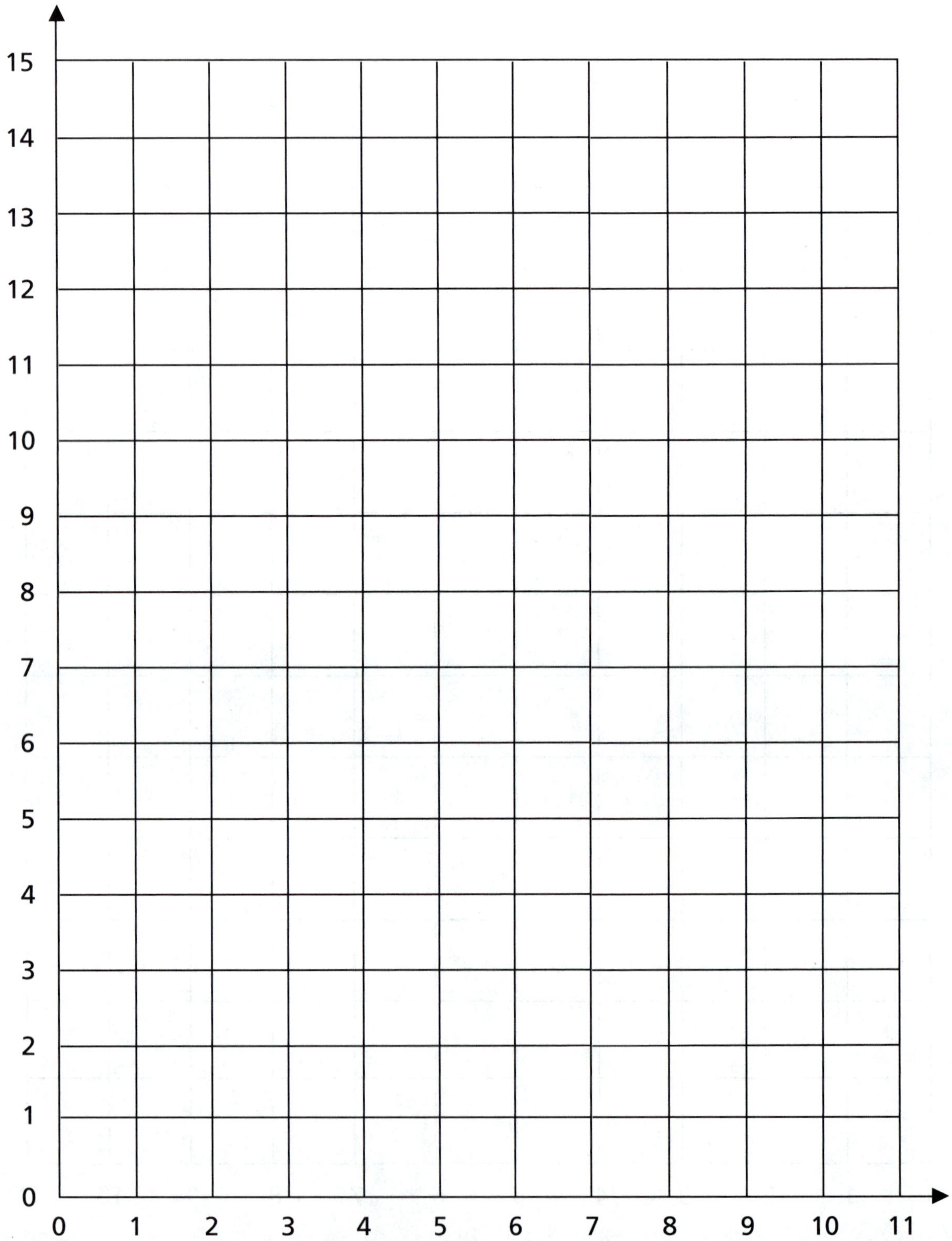

Name ______________________________

THE PICTURED COORDINATES

Write the coordinates of each point of your drawing. Write the points in order, from one to the next, following the line segments of your drawing. Use as many points as you need—feel free to write more. Give this page to your partner.

1. (___, ___)	2. (___, ___)	3. (___, ___)	4. (___, ___)
5. (___, ___)	6. (___, ___)	7. (___, ___)	8. (___, ___)
9. (___, ___)	10. (___, ___)	11. (___, ___)	12. (___, ___)
13. (___, ___)	14. (___, ___)	15. (___, ___)	16. (___, ___)
17. (___, ___)	18. (___, ___)	19. (___, ___)	20. (___, ___)
21. (___, ___)	22. (___, ___)	23. (___, ___)	24. (___, ___)
25. (___, ___)	26. (___, ___)	27. (___, ___)	28. (___, ___)
29. (___, ___)	30. (___, ___)	31. (___, ___)	32. (___, ___)
33. (___, ___)	34. (___, ___)	35. (___, ___)	36. (___, ___)
37. (___, ___)	38. (___, ___)	39. (___, ___)	40. (___, ___)

MYSTERY ART

Use the coordinates of your partner's drawing to reproduce it. Draw a point at the location of each coordinate pair. Then draw line segments connecting the points in the same order they are given. Does your reproduction match the original?

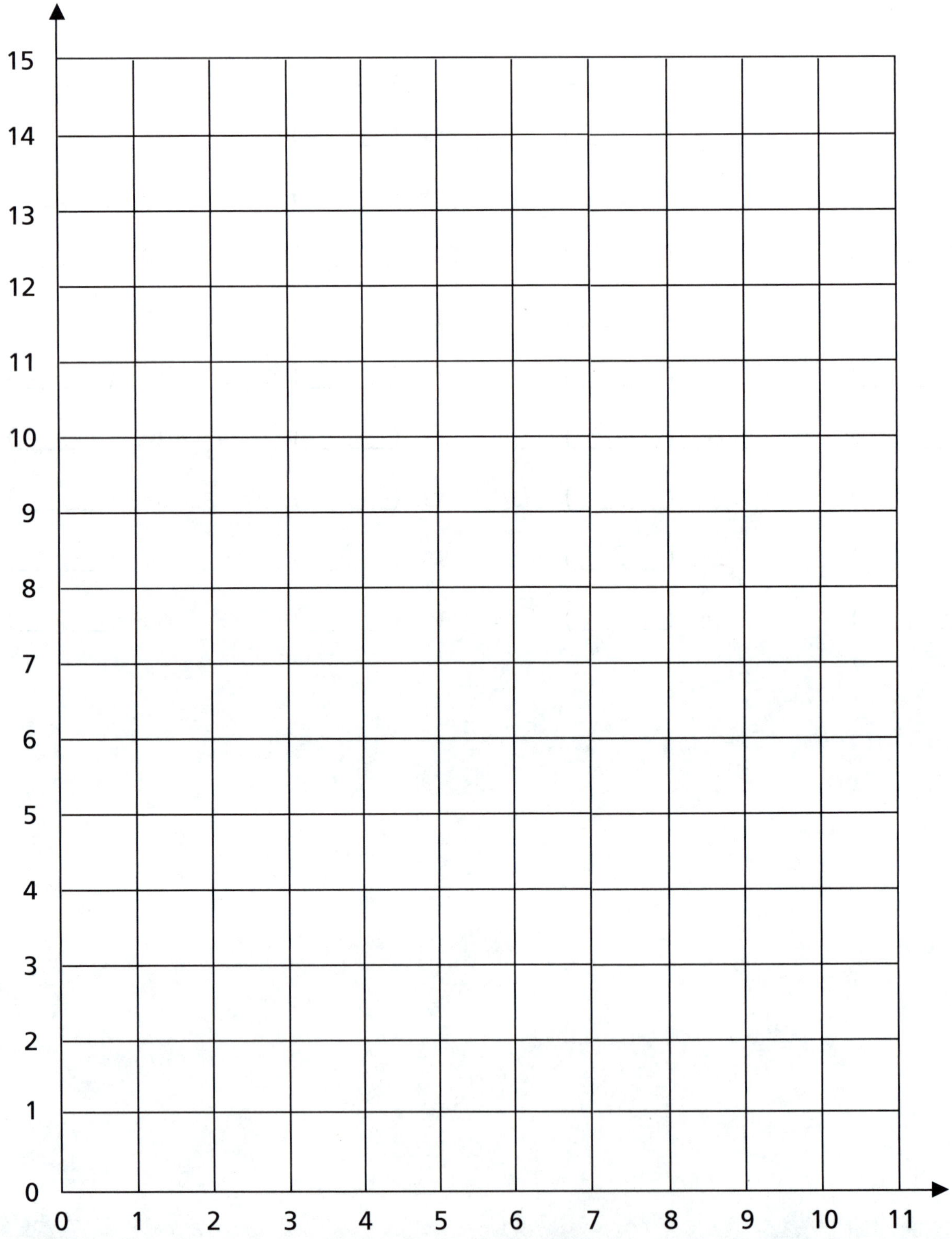

Name ____________________

HOME CONNECTION: GOING BOWLING

Dear Parent or Guardian:

Your child has been learning how to find and plot points on a coordinate grid. In this assignment, your child will create a path on a coordinate grid map. Then he or she will write directions for following the path, such as *Go to (3, 6). Now go to (0, 6)*. See if you can follow your child's path!

Draw a path from Gigaplex Movies to Universal Bowling. Use only line segments that end at the intersection of two grid lines.

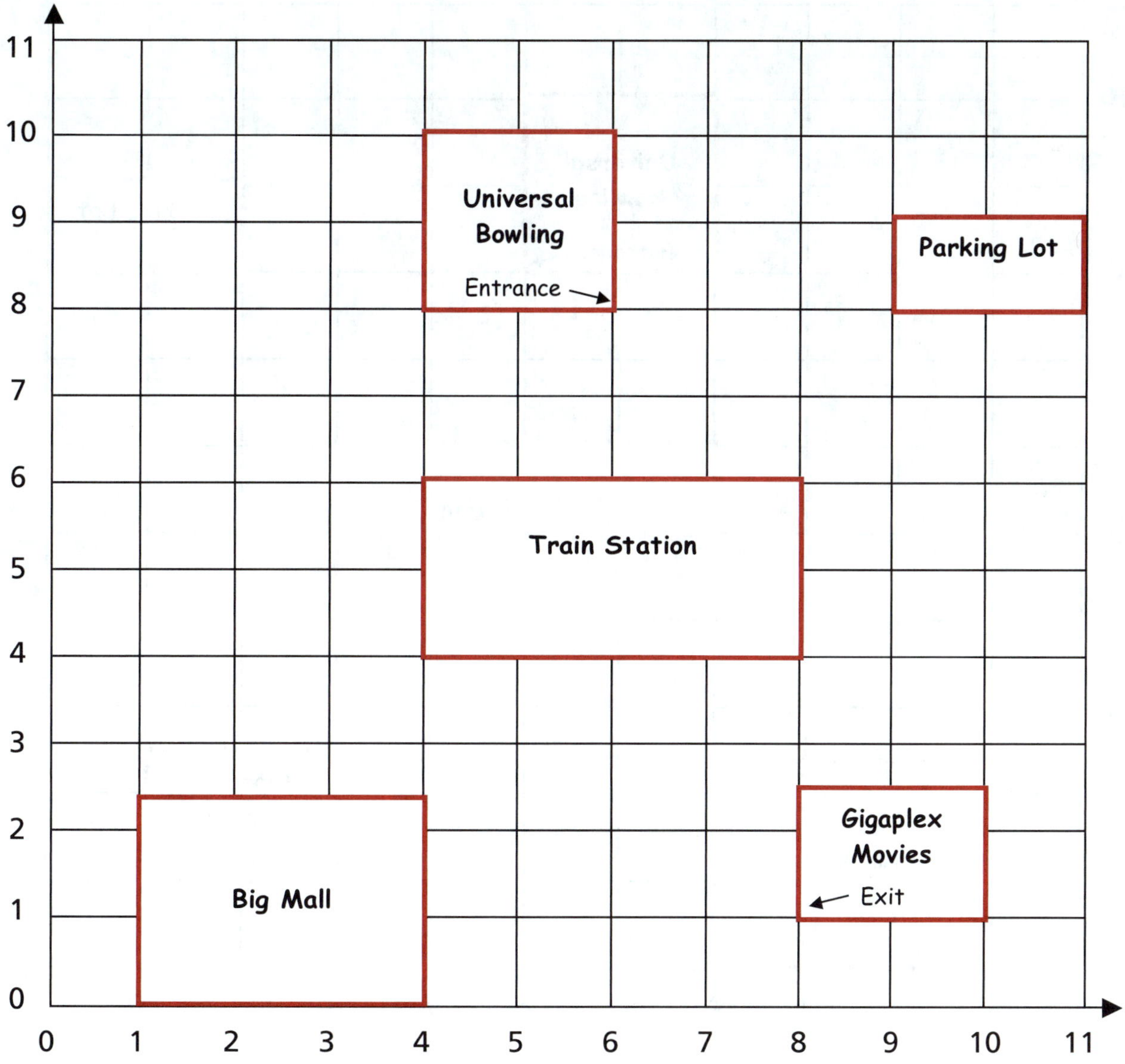

Write the coordinates of each point on your path from Gigaplex Movies to Universal Bowling. Give this page to your parent or guardian. Ask him or her to reproduce your path—without peeking at your original map!

Directions:

____

____

____

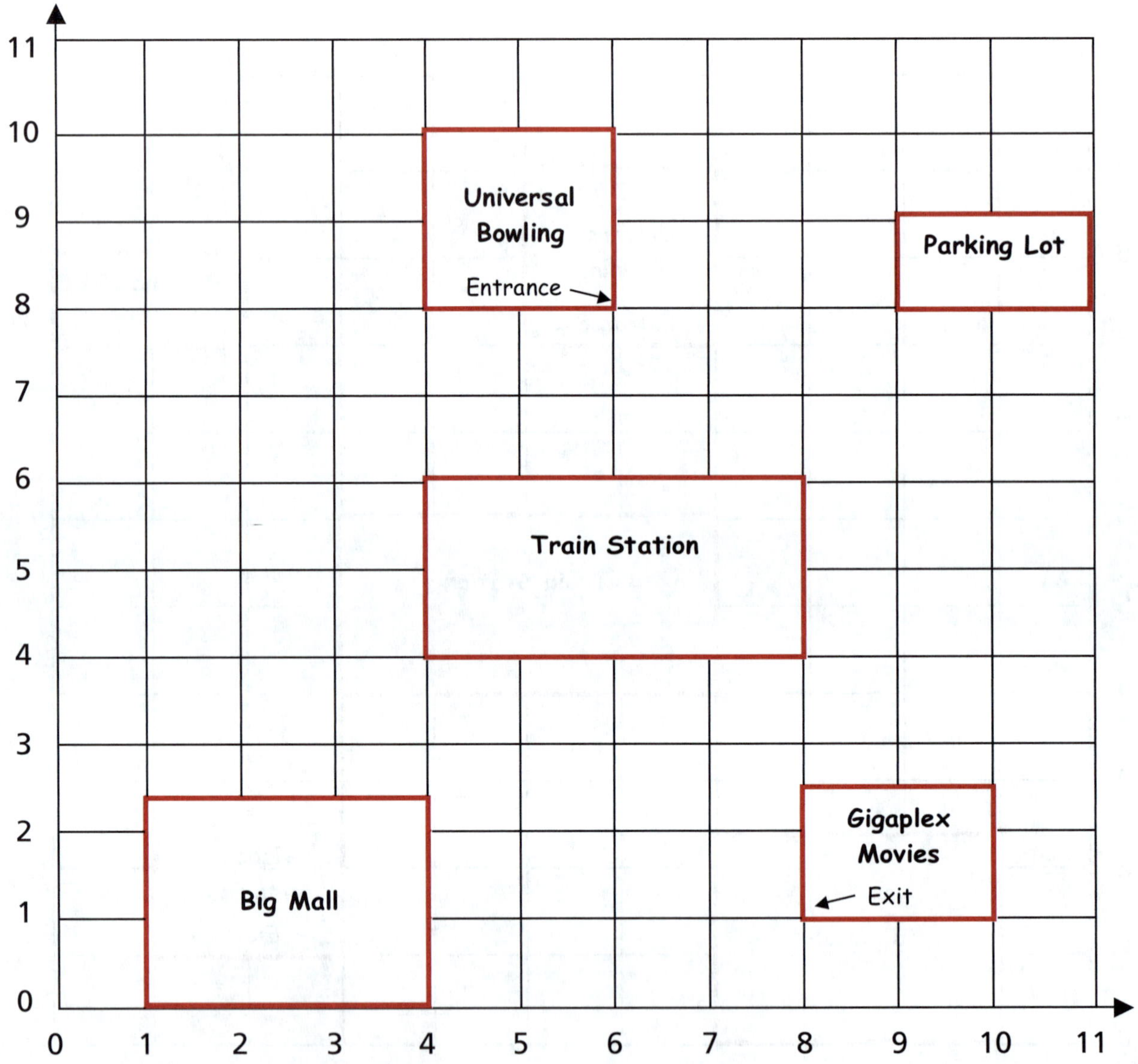

Name ____

Works of The Puzzler

THE PUZZLER'S TRIANGLES WITHIN TRIANGLES

Figure 1

Figure 2

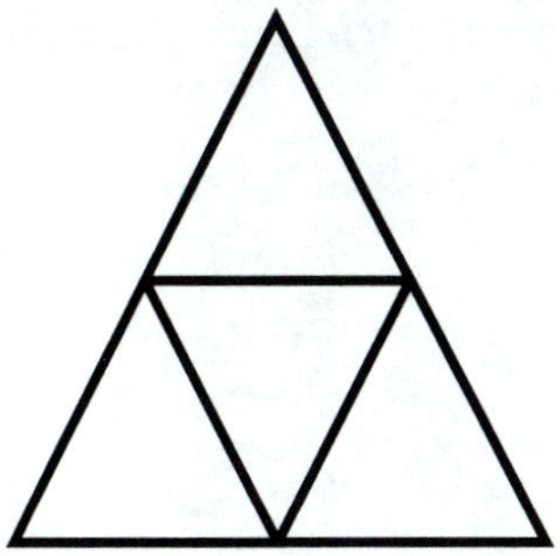

Figure 3

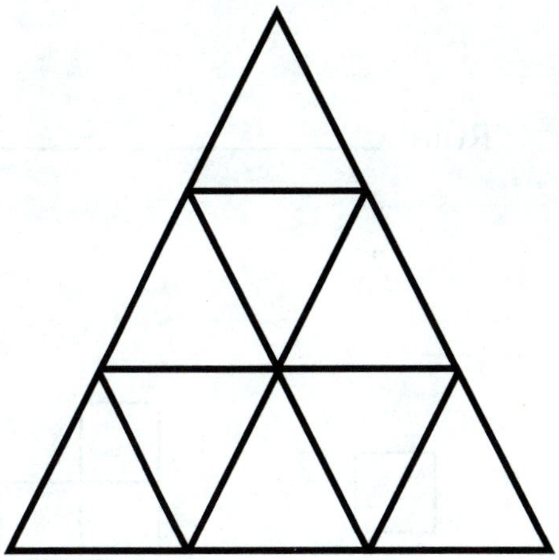

Figure 4

?

FINDING THE PUZZLER'S PATTERNS

Use square tiles to complete The Puzzler's patterns. Draw the next piece and write the rule.

1.

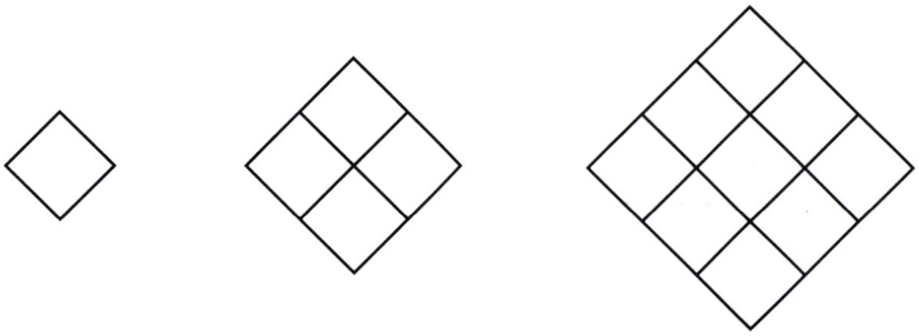

Rule: ______________________________

2.

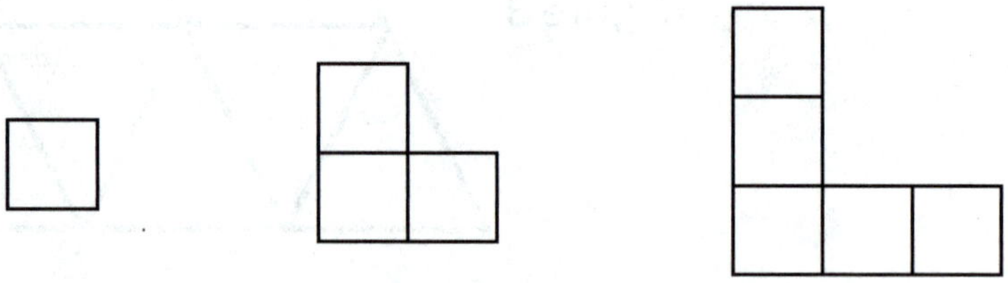

Rule: ______________________________

3.

Rule: ______________________________

Name ____________________

RULES AND PATTERNS

Write the next 3 numbers or letters in the patterns. Then write a rule for the pattern. If you can, use a variable to write the rule.

Example: **1, 2, 3, 4, <u>5</u>, <u>6</u>, <u>7</u>, . . .** **Rule:** $n + 1$

1. 1, 3, 5, 7, ____, ____, ____, . . . Rule: ____________

2. 1, 2, 4, 8, ____, ____, ____, . . . Rule: ____________

3. 3, 9, 27, ____, ____, ____, . . . Rule: ____________

4. 0, 5, 10, 15, ____, ____, ____, . . . Rule: ____________

5. A, C, E, G, ____, ____, ____, . . . Rule: ____________

6. 1, 10, 100, ______, ______, ______, . . . Rule: ____________

Using a variable, write a rule for each pattern.

7. 

Rule: ____________

8. 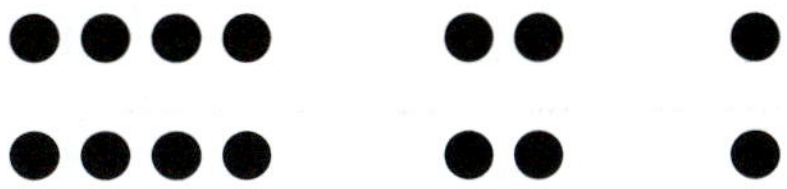

Rule: ____________

THE PUZZLER'S CIRCLES OF THOUGHT

Draw the next two figures in The Puzzler's pattern. Then write a rule for the pattern.

Figure 1

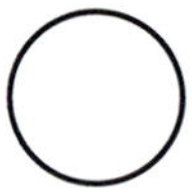

Figure 2

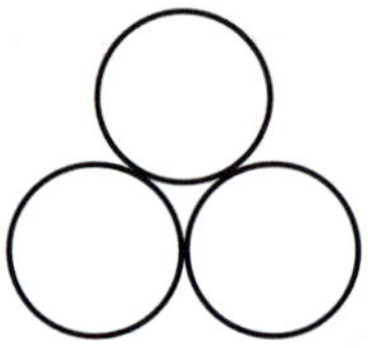

Figure 3

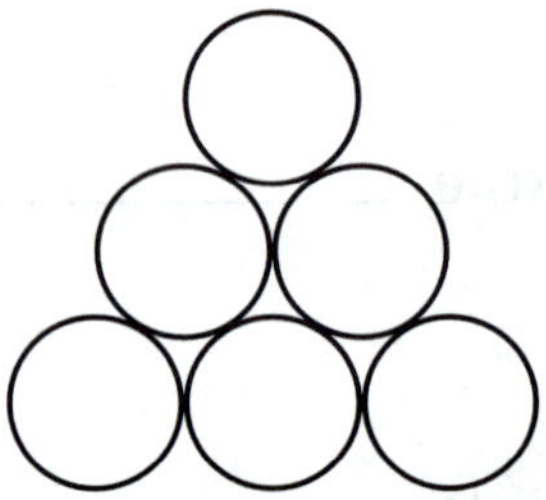

Figure 4

?

Figure 5

?

Rule: ____

____

Name ____

HOME CONNECTION: PUZZLING PATTERNS

Dear Parent or Guardian:

Your child has been learning about patterns in sequences of numbers and in sequences of geometric shapes. Please help your child solve the problems on the next page.

Write the next 3 numbers in the sequence. Then write a rule for the pattern. If you can, use a variable for the rule.

1. 90, 85, 80, 75, ______, ______, ______, . . . Rule: ____________________

2. 2, 6, 18, ______, ______, ______, . . . Rule: ____________________

3. D, G, J, M, ______, ______, ______, . . . Rule: ____________________

4. 2, 5, 15, 18, 28, ______, ______, ______, . . . Rule: ____________________

5. 44, 40, 39, 35, 34, ______, ______, ______, . . . Rule: ____________________

6. 3, 10, 17, 24, ______, ______, ______, . . . Rule: ____________________

Using a variable, write a rule for the pattern.

7. Rule: ____________________

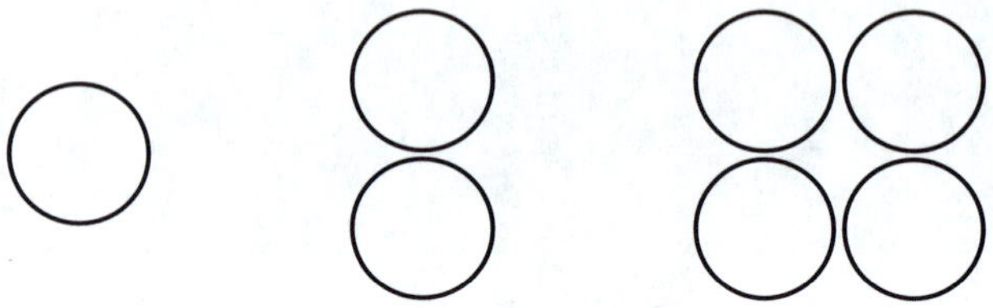

8. Rule: ____________________

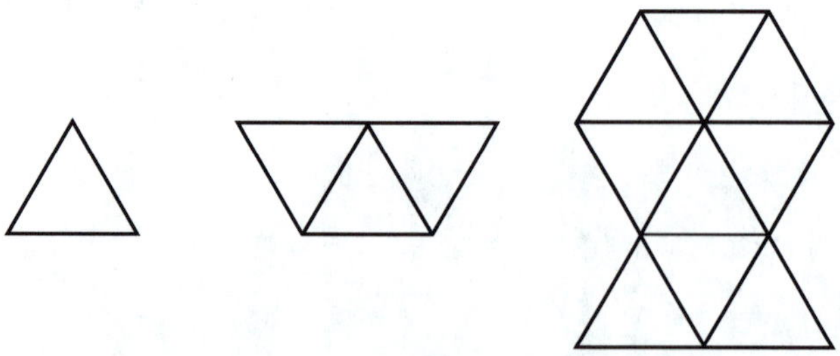

Name ______________________________

Pump Up the Volume

BUILD A BOX

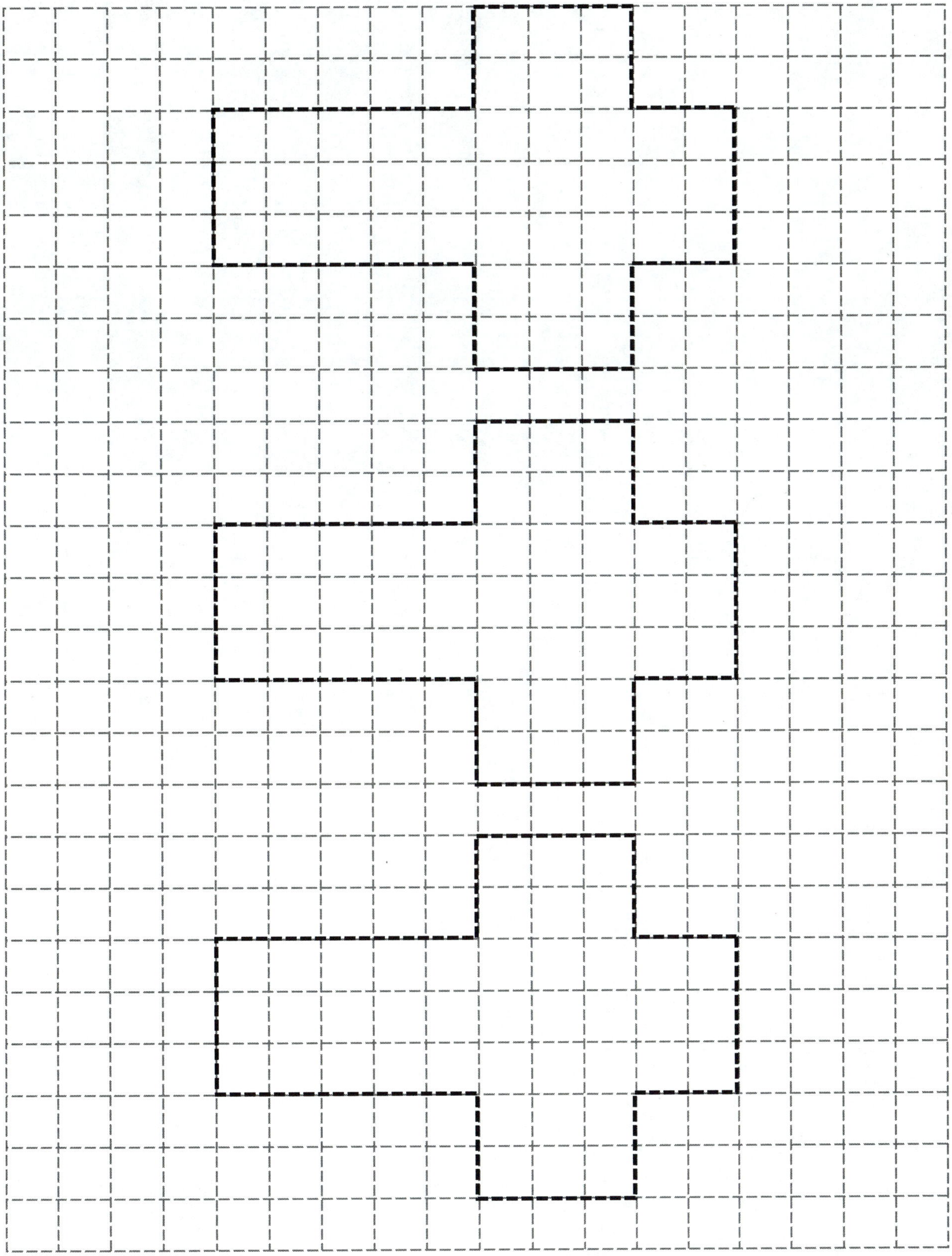

Name ______________________________

WHAT'S ITS VOLUME?

Look at each box.
Predict the volume.
Record your prediction.
Build the box using centimeter cubes.
Determine and record the actual volume.
Find the difference between your prediction and the actual volume.

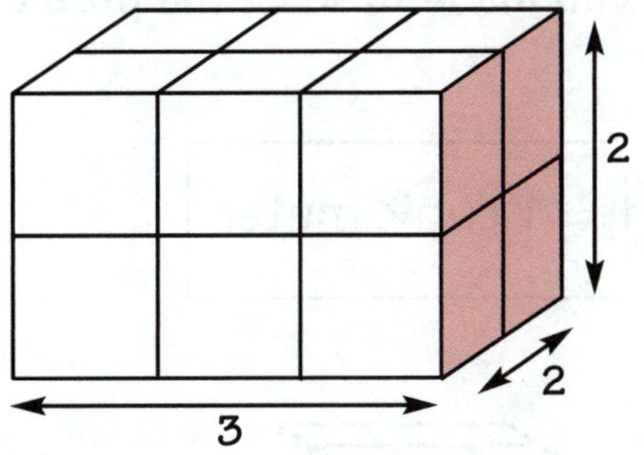

1.

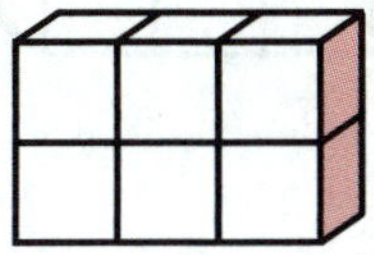

Prediction: __________

Actual: __________

Difference: __________

2.

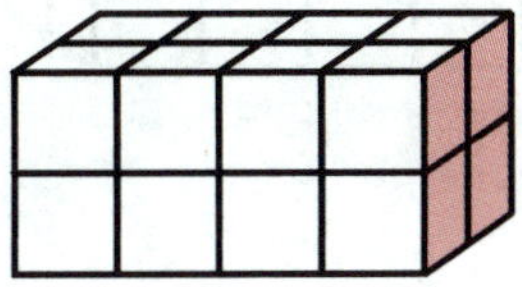

Prediction: __________

Actual: __________

Difference: __________

3.

Prediction: __________

Actual: __________

Difference: __________

4.

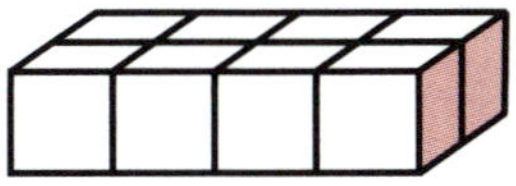

Prediction: __________

Actual: __________

Difference: __________

5.

Prediction: __________

Actual: __________

Difference: __________

6.

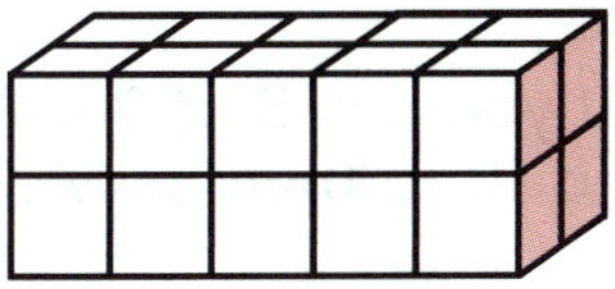

Prediction: __________

Actual: __________

Difference: __________

HEY KIDS . . . IT'S THE STORAGE ROOM!

Mo owns a storage room. The volume of his storage room is 80 cubic meters. Use that information, the boxes below, and the box you made to solve the problems.

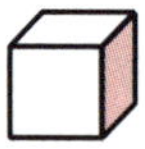 = 1 cubic meter

B

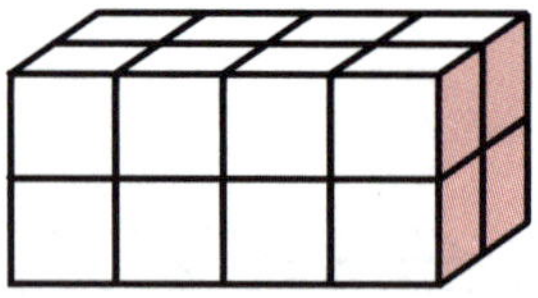

C

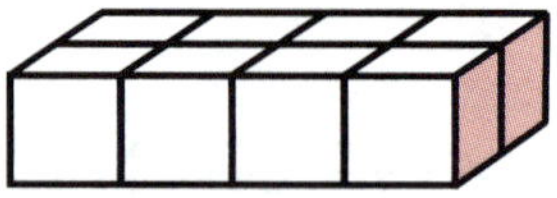

D

E

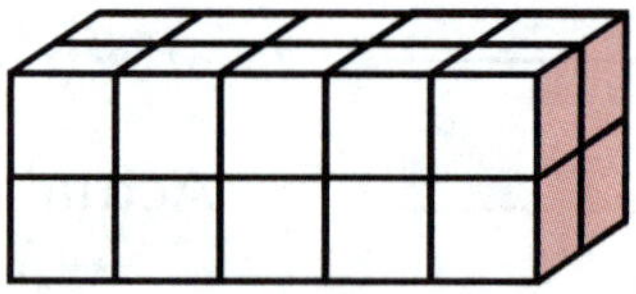

F

1. If you had 3 of Box E and 2 of Box A, would you be able to store them in Mo's storage room? Explain.

2. How many of Box F would fit in Mo's storage room?

3. Joey says that 10 of a certain box will fit exactly in Mo's storage room. Which box is Joey talking about?

4. If Maggie needed to store 6 of Box A and 4 of Box B, would she be able to use Mo's storage room?

Name ______________________________

HOME CONNECTION: PUMP UP THE VOLUME

Dear Parent or Guardian:

Your child has been learning about the volume of objects. Please help your child use the grid on the next page to design, cut out, and build a box. The box should have a volume of 24 cubic units; it should also have a lid. **Hint:** It may be easier for your child to build the box with the gridlines on the outside of the box.

TOPIC 6

Fractions and Mixed Numbers

Name ______________________________

Looks Aren't Deceiving

FRACTION STRIPS

Cut out each fraction strip.

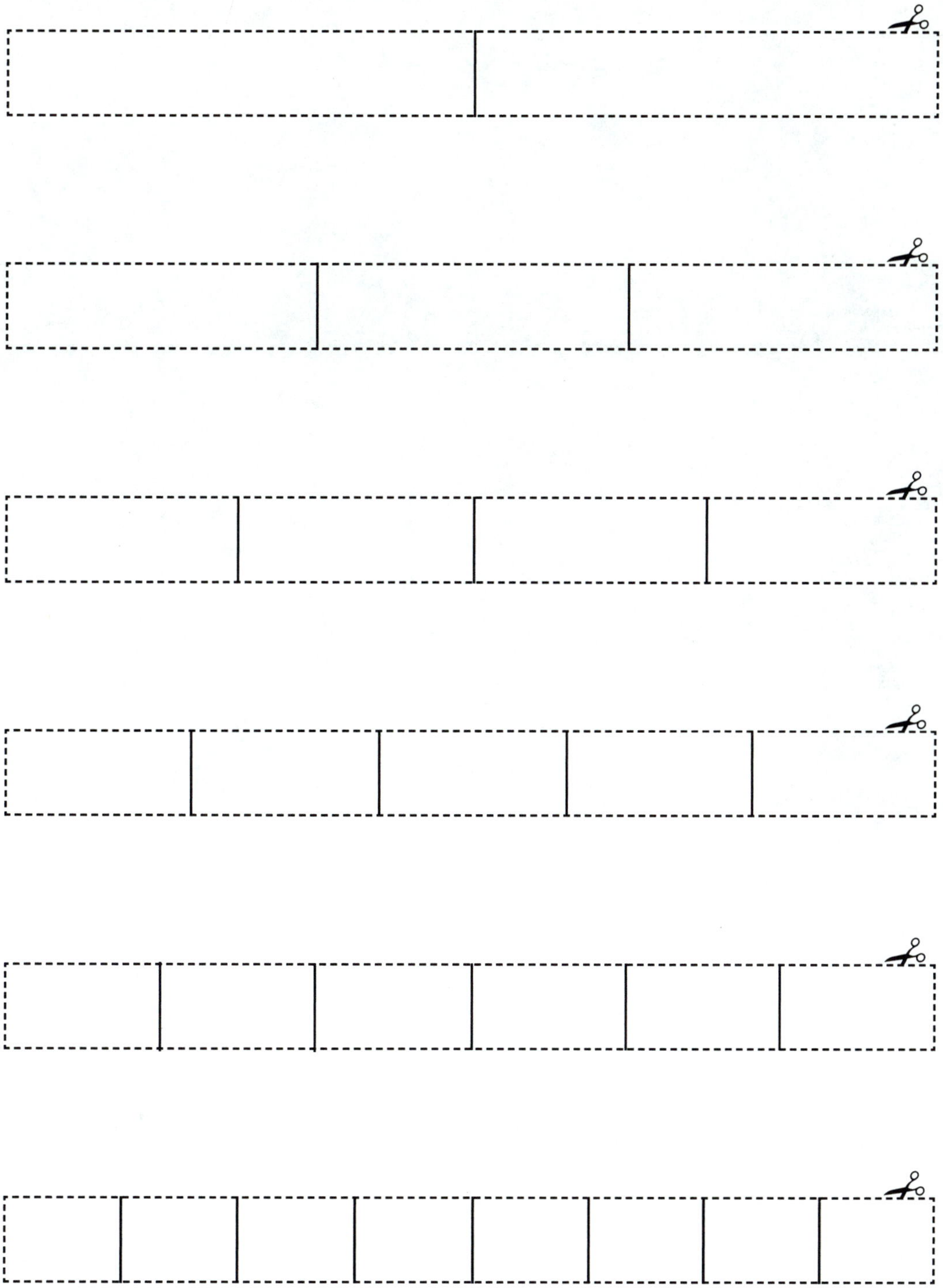

Name ______________________________

THE EQUIVALENCE OF FRACTIONS

Use your fraction strips to determine whether the fractions are equivalent. Circle *equivalent* or *not equivalent*.

1.	$\frac{1}{4}$ and $\frac{1}{3}$	equivalent	not equivalent
2.	$\frac{3}{6}$ and $\frac{3}{8}$	equivalent	not equivalent
3.	$\frac{1}{3}$ and $\frac{2}{6}$	equivalent	not equivalent
4.	$\frac{4}{5}$ and $\frac{6}{8}$	equivalent	not equivalent
5.	$\frac{2}{4}$ and $\frac{1}{2}$	equivalent	not equivalent
6.	$\frac{2}{8}$ and $\frac{1}{4}$	equivalent	not equivalent
7.	$\frac{2}{3}$ and $\frac{3}{5}$	equivalent	not equivalent
8.	$\frac{3}{6}$ and $\frac{4}{8}$	equivalent	not equivalent
9.	$\frac{6}{8}$ and $\frac{3}{4}$	equivalent	not equivalent
10.	$\frac{4}{6}$ and $\frac{4}{5}$	equivalent	not equivalent

FRACTIONS ON NUMBER LINES

Use your fraction strips to draw a point at the fraction. Write the fraction under the point.

1. $\frac{1}{5}$ 0 ———————— 1

2. $\frac{3}{6}$ 0 ———————— 1

3. $\frac{7}{8}$ 0 ———————— 1

4. $\frac{2}{3}$ 0 ———————— 1

5. $\frac{2}{6}$ 0 ———————— 1

6. $\frac{1}{2}$ 0 ———————— 1

7. $\frac{2}{4}$ 0 ———————— 1

8. $\frac{1}{3}$ 0 ———————— 1

9. $\frac{3}{4}$ 0 ———————— 1

10. $\frac{3}{5}$ 0 ———————— 1

Name ______________________________

RECTANGLES OF EQUIVALENCE

1. Shade $\frac{1}{2}$ of each rectangle. Write the equivalent fractions.
Draw lines across the last rectangle to show your own equivalent fraction.

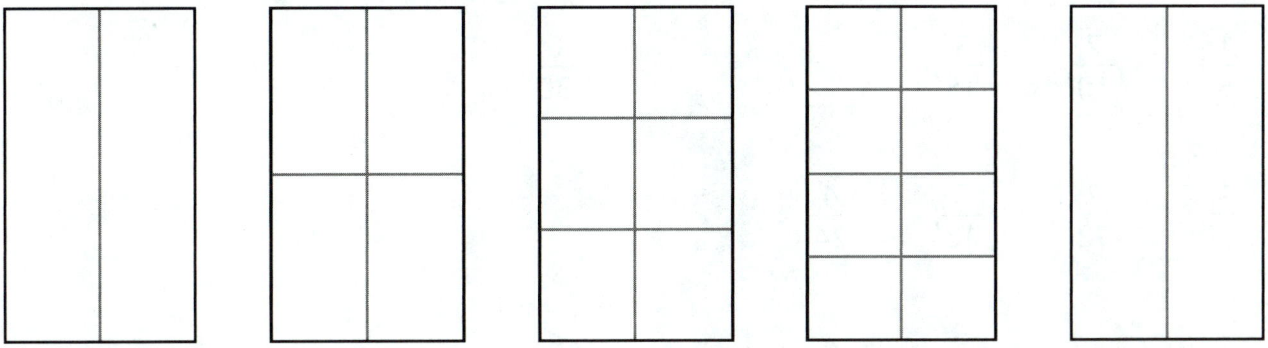

$\frac{1}{2}$ = = = =

2. Shade $\frac{1}{3}$ of each rectangle. Write the equivalent fractions.
Draw lines across the last rectangle to show your own equivalent fraction.

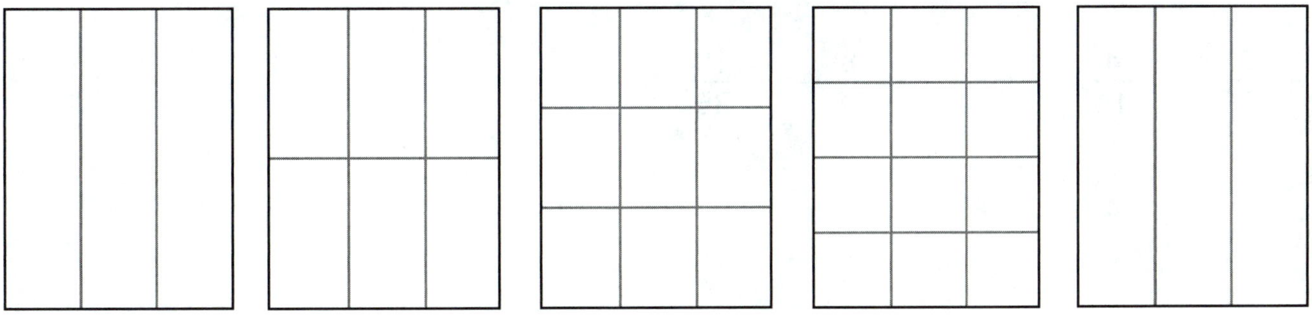

$\frac{1}{3}$ = = = =

3. Shade $\frac{1}{4}$ of each rectangle. Write the equivalent fractions.
Draw lines across the last rectangle to show your own equivalent fraction.

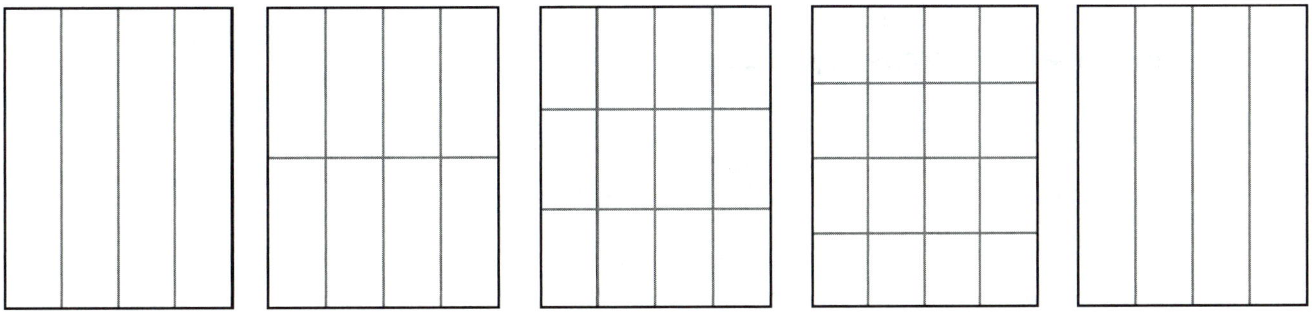

$\frac{1}{4}$ = = = =

FRACTION PATTERNS

Write equivalent fractions to complete the pattern.

1.	$\frac{1}{2}$,	$\frac{2}{4}$,	$\frac{3}{6}$,		$\frac{5}{10}$,	
2.	$\frac{1}{5}$,	$\frac{2}{10}$,	$\frac{3}{15}$,			$\frac{6}{30}$
3.	$\frac{1}{6}$,	$\frac{2}{12}$,	$\frac{3}{18}$,	$\frac{4}{24}$,		
4.	$\frac{1}{3}$,		$\frac{3}{9}$,	$\frac{4}{12}$,		$\frac{6}{18}$
5.	$\frac{2}{5}$,	$\frac{4}{10}$,	$\frac{6}{15}$,		$\frac{10}{25}$,	
6.	$\frac{2}{7}$,	$\frac{4}{14}$,		$\frac{8}{28}$,	$\frac{10}{35}$,	
7.	$\frac{2}{3}$,	$\frac{4}{6}$,	$\frac{6}{9}$,			$\frac{12}{18}$

8. Describe the pattern in problem 7.

The numerators increase by______s.

The denominators increase by______s.

Name ____

HOME CONNECTION: HANDSPANS

Dear Parent or Guardian:

Your child has been learning how to find and write equivalent fractions. Equivalent fractions, such as $\frac{1}{2}$ and $\frac{2}{4}$, have the same value. In class, your child made a ruler with his or her "handspan"—the distance from the tip of the thumb to the tip of the fifth finger—as the unit. The ruler is separated into eighths. With your help, your child will measure some objects around the house, state each measurement as a fraction of a handspan, and then write the measurement using an equivalent fraction.

HANDSPANS

Measure the length, width, or height of six objects. Measure objects that are shorter than your handspan. Name the object and write its measurement. Then write the measurement using an equivalent fraction.

Example: Object: *toy car*
Measurement: $\frac{1}{4}$ *handspan*
Measurement with equivalent fraction: $\frac{2}{8}$ *handspan*

1. Object:
   Measurement:
   Measurement with equivalent fraction:

2. Object:
   Measurement:
   Measurement with equivalent fraction:

3. Object:
   Measurement:
   Measurement with equivalent fraction:

4. Object:
   Measurement:
   Measurement with equivalent fraction:

5. Object:
   Measurement:
   Measurement with equivalent fraction:

6. Object:
   Measurement:
   Measurement with equivalent fraction:

Name ____________________

FRACTION STRIPS

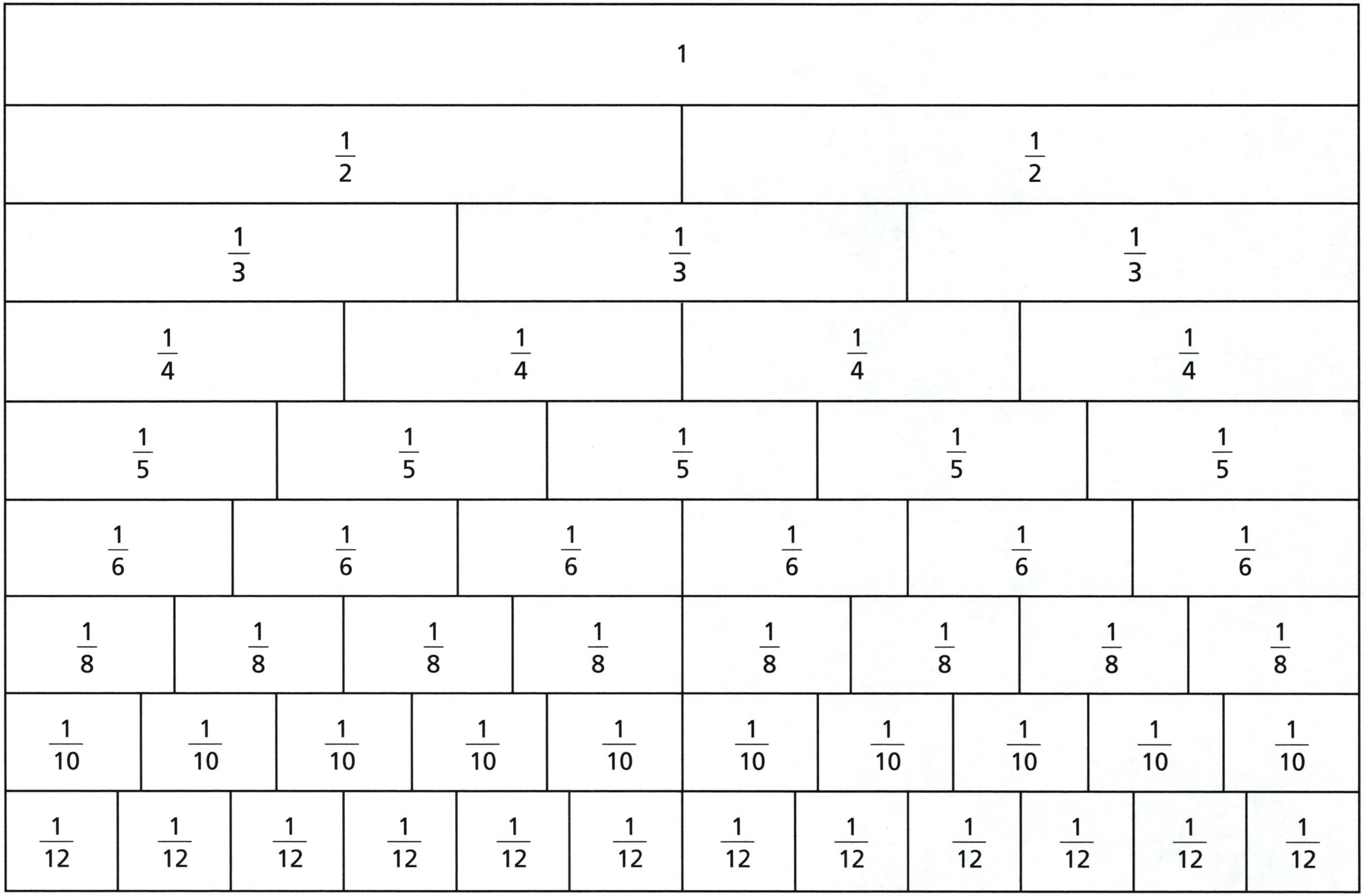

Name ______________________________

GAME PIECES

$\frac{1}{1}$	$\frac{1}{2}$	$\frac{1}{3}$	$\frac{2}{3}$	$\frac{5}{6}$
$\frac{1}{4}$	$\frac{2}{4}$	$\frac{3}{4}$	$\frac{1}{5}$	$\frac{4}{8}$
$\frac{2}{5}$	$\frac{3}{5}$	$\frac{4}{5}$	$\frac{1}{6}$	$\frac{1}{10}$
$\frac{2}{10}$	$\frac{3}{10}$	$\frac{4}{10}$	$\frac{5}{10}$	$\frac{2}{6}$
$\frac{6}{10}$	$\frac{7}{10}$	$\frac{8}{10}$	$\frac{9}{10}$	$\frac{1}{8}$
$\frac{1}{12}$	$\frac{2}{12}$	$\frac{3}{12}$	$\frac{4}{12}$	$\frac{5}{8}$
$\frac{5}{12}$	$\frac{6}{12}$	$\frac{7}{12}$	$\frac{8}{12}$	$\frac{11}{12}$

Name ______________________________

$\frac{9}{12}$	$\frac{10}{12}$	$\frac{4}{6}$	$\frac{7}{8}$	$\frac{2}{8}$
$\frac{12}{12}$	$\frac{3}{8}$	$\frac{3}{6}$	$\frac{6}{8}$	

Fractions: The Same, More or Less Game Board

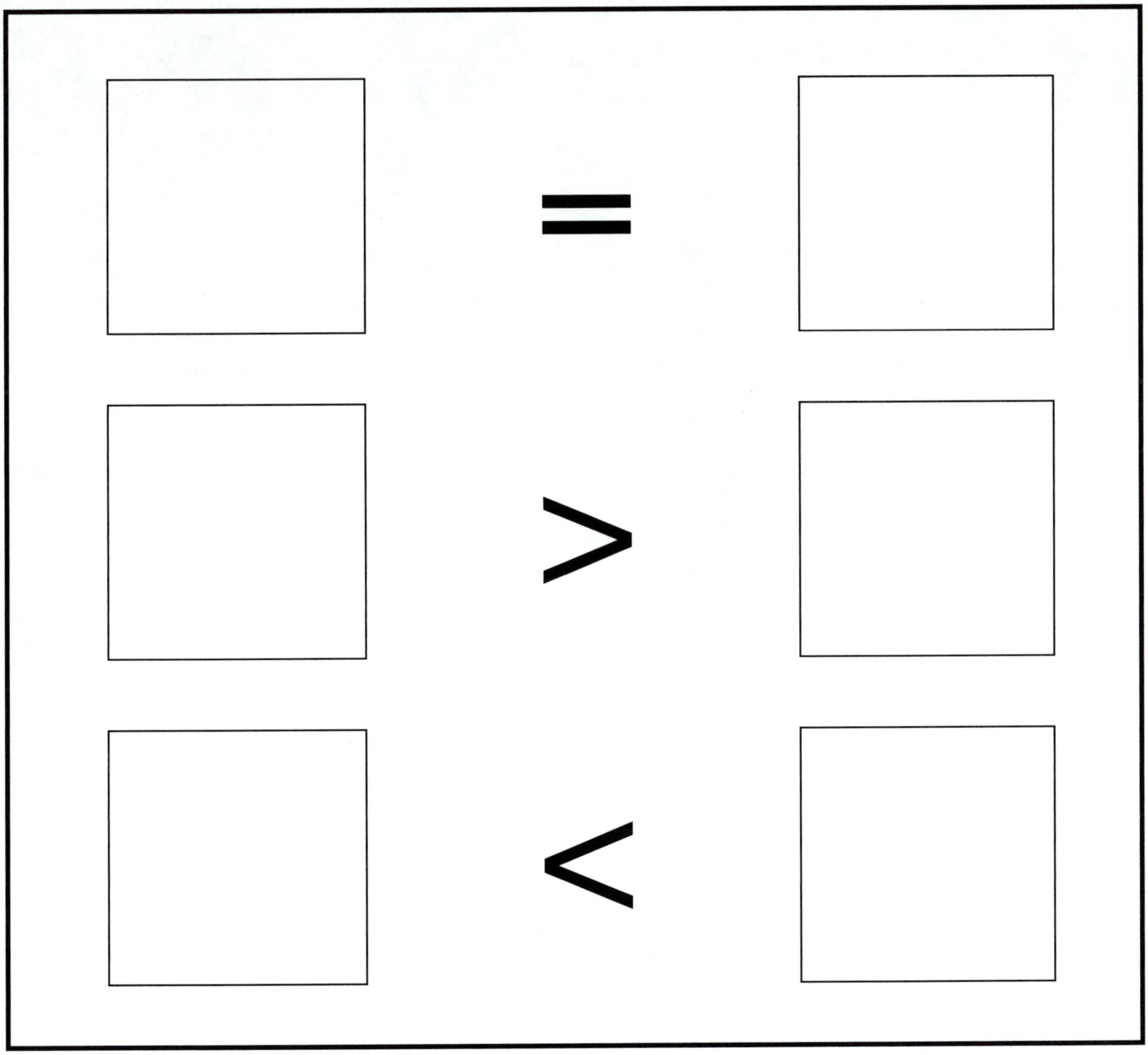

Name ____________________

FRACTION FACE-OFF CHECK CHART

1

$\frac{1}{2}$ $\frac{1}{2}$

$\frac{1}{3}$ $\frac{1}{3}$ $\frac{1}{3}$

$\frac{1}{4}$ $\frac{1}{4}$ $\frac{1}{4}$ $\frac{1}{4}$

$\frac{1}{5}$ $\frac{1}{5}$ $\frac{1}{5}$ $\frac{1}{5}$ $\frac{1}{5}$

$\frac{1}{6}$ $\frac{1}{6}$ $\frac{1}{6}$ $\frac{1}{6}$ $\frac{1}{6}$ $\frac{1}{6}$

$\frac{1}{8}$ $\frac{1}{8}$ $\frac{1}{8}$ $\frac{1}{8}$ $\frac{1}{8}$ $\frac{1}{8}$ $\frac{1}{8}$ $\frac{1}{8}$

$\frac{1}{10}$ $\frac{1}{10}$ $\frac{1}{10}$ $\frac{1}{10}$ $\frac{1}{10}$ $\frac{1}{10}$ $\frac{1}{10}$ $\frac{1}{10}$ $\frac{1}{10}$ $\frac{1}{10}$

$\frac{1}{12}$ $\frac{1}{12}$ $\frac{1}{12}$ $\frac{1}{12}$ $\frac{1}{12}$ $\frac{1}{12}$ $\frac{1}{12}$ $\frac{1}{12}$ $\frac{1}{12}$ $\frac{1}{12}$ $\frac{1}{12}$ $\frac{1}{12}$

SHAWN'S COLLECTION CHOICES

Most Wanted	→					Least Wanted
1st choice	2nd choice	3rd choice	4th choice	5th choice	6th choice	7th choice
Collection of Toy Cars	Collection of Shark Teeth	Collection of Baseball Cards	Collection of Coins	Collection of Fossils	Collection of Old Records	Collection of Rubber Bands

Name ______________________________

HOME CONNECTION: GREATER THAN, LESS THAN, EQUAL

Dear Parent or Guardian:

Your child has been using fraction circles and fraction strips to learn about comparing and ordering fractions. Your child has been working with halves, thirds, fourths, fifths, sixths, eighths, tenths, and twelfths.

For this activity, help your child with solving the inequalities and equalities on the reverse side of this page. Your child can use the fraction strips printed at the top of the page for help.

- **Write <, >, or = for each pair of fractions.**
- **Use the fraction strips at the top of the page for help.**

FRACTIONS

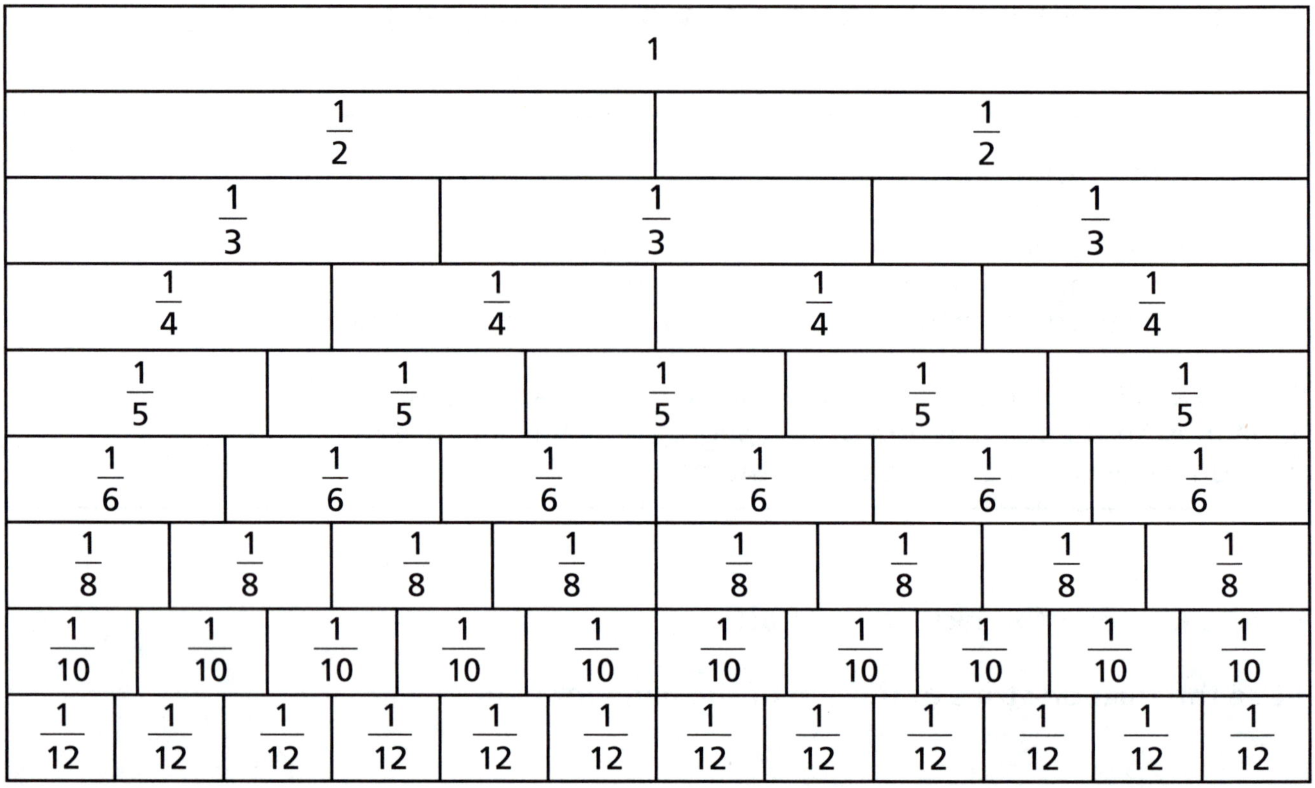

Compare the fractions. Write <, >, or =.

1. $\frac{1}{2} \bigcirc \frac{2}{5}$

2. $\frac{3}{6} \bigcirc \frac{4}{8}$

3. $\frac{7}{12} \bigcirc \frac{6}{8}$

4. $\frac{2}{5} \bigcirc \frac{2}{3}$

5. $\frac{2}{3} \bigcirc \frac{4}{6}$

6. $\frac{3}{10} \bigcirc \frac{1}{3}$

7. $\frac{11}{12} \bigcirc \frac{7}{8}$

8. $\frac{7}{10} \bigcirc \frac{3}{4}$

9. $\frac{3}{8} \bigcirc \frac{1}{3}$

10. $\frac{4}{12} \bigcirc \frac{1}{3}$

Name ______________________________

Frac Attack

FRACTION STRIP

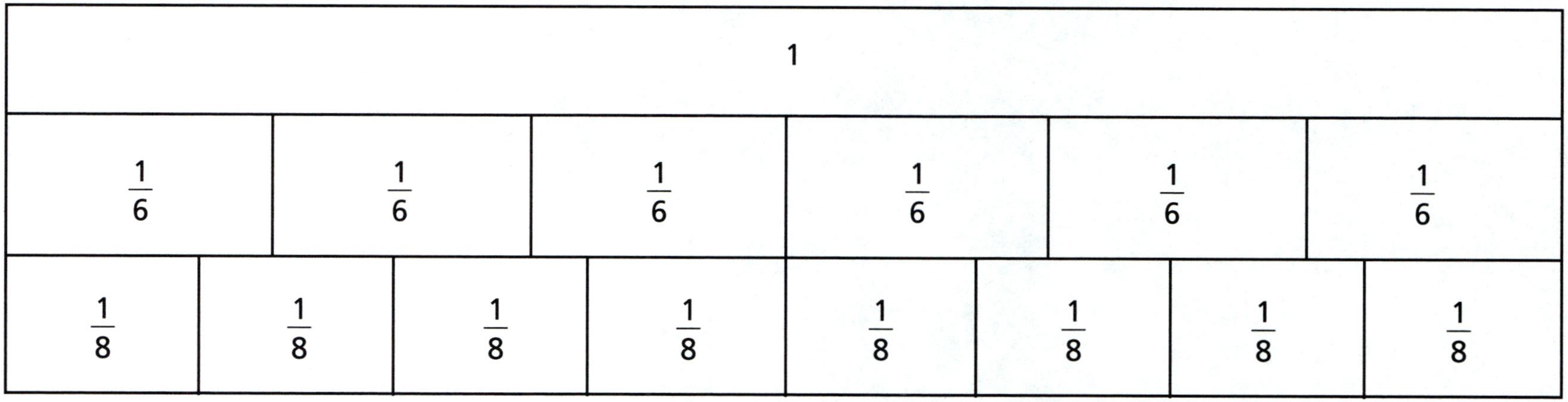

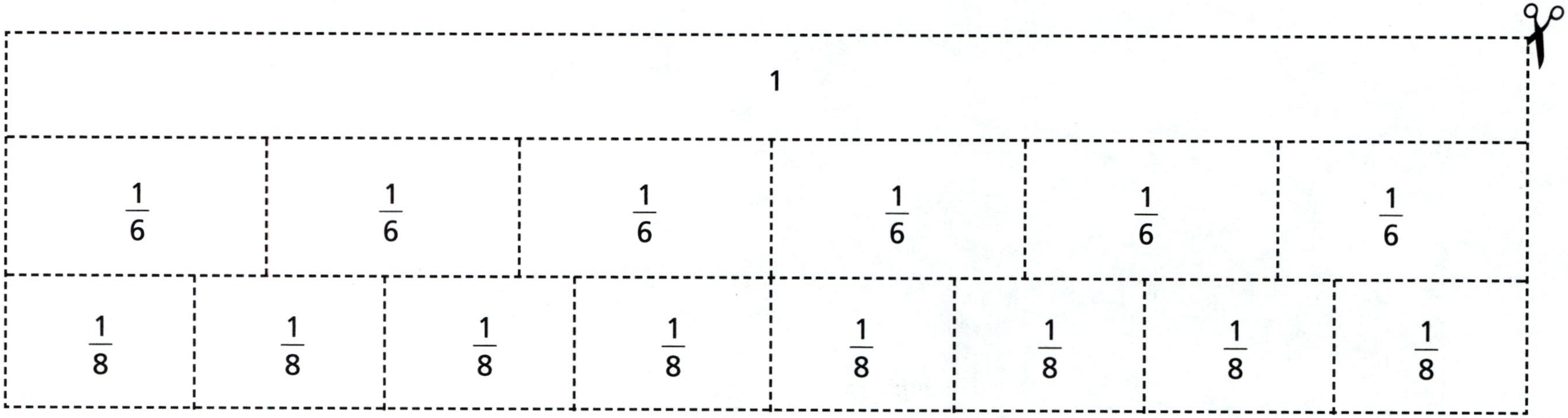

Name ____________________

ADD AND SUBTRACT FRACTIONS

Write a number sentence for each item. Then solve the item. Problems may need two steps to solve.

1. Sarah's family bought a pizza for dinner. The pizza was cut into 6 pieces. Sarah ate 1 piece. Her brother ate 2 pieces. What fraction of the pizza is left?

2. Ms. Griffin's class has 16 students. During lunch, $\frac{7}{16}$ of the class ate spaghetti and $\frac{5}{16}$ of the class ate corn dogs. The rest of the class brought their lunches. What fraction of the class ate spaghetti or corn dogs? What fraction of the class brought their lunches?

3. In a snail race, Jackie's snail moves $\frac{2}{8}$ inch in the first minute. In the next minute, the snail moves $\frac{3}{8}$ inch. How much farther does Jackie's snail have to move to reach 1 inch?

4. Karen is growing a plant for a science experiment. In the first two weeks, Karen's plant grows $\frac{3}{12}$ foot. In the next two weeks, her plant grows $\frac{4}{12}$ foot. How tall is the plant? How much more must the plant grow to reach 1 foot?

5. Trina and Ed share a submarine sandwich. Trina cuts the sandwich into 9 equal pieces. She eats $\frac{2}{9}$ of the sandwich. Ed eats $\frac{2}{9}$, too. How much of the sandwich did Trina and Ed eat? How much of the sandwich is left?

EATING FRACTIONS

Use the following information to help you write number sentences or expressions to solve the items.

Mr. Rotolo made a homemade pizza for his family of four. Mr. Rotolo made sure that $\frac{6}{12}$ of the pizza was pepperoni and the other $\frac{6}{12}$ was plain cheese. He cut the pizza into 12 equal servings.

1. Mr. Rotolo was the first person to try out his delicious creation. Before dinner, he ate one slice from the pepperoni side of the pizza. What fraction of the pizza was left?

2. At dinner, Mr. Rotolo ate one more slice from the pepperoni side of the pizza. What fractional part of the pizza was now left?

3. Sandy, Mr. Rotolo's daughter, ate $\frac{3}{12}$ of the original pizza for dinner and her brother Hector ate $\frac{4}{12}$ of the original pizza. What fraction of the original pizza did Sandy and her brother eat together?

4. Write an expression to show that Hector ate more pizza than Sandy did.

5. Sandy only eats plain cheese pizza and Hector only eats pepperoni pizza. Sandy ate 3 slices. What fractional part of the cheese pizza is left? **Hint:** Remember only half the pizza is cheese pizza.

6. After Mr. Rotolo, Sandy, and Hector ate their slices, Mrs. Rotolo ate $\frac{3}{12}$ of the pizza. How much of the pizza was remaining after dinner? Explain.

Name ____________________

HOME CONNECTION: FRACTION FUN

Dear Parent or Guardian:

Your child has been learning to add and subtract fractions. He or she has been using fraction strips such as the ones below to solve word problems. Have your child cut out the fraction strips and use them to solve the problems given below. Then on the reverse side of this page, your child will write his or her own word problem requiring the addition or subtraction of fractions.

Cut out the fraction strips. Use them to solve these problems. Then write your own fraction word problem. Your word problem should require addition or subtraction of fractions.

1. $\frac{4}{6} - \frac{3}{6} =$

2. $\frac{5}{8} - \frac{2}{8} =$

3. $\frac{1}{6} + \frac{4}{6} =$

4. $\frac{5}{8} - \frac{2}{8} =$

1

$\frac{1}{6}$	$\frac{1}{6}$	$\frac{1}{6}$	$\frac{1}{6}$	$\frac{1}{6}$	$\frac{1}{6}$

$\frac{1}{8}$	$\frac{1}{8}$	$\frac{1}{8}$	$\frac{1}{8}$	$\frac{1}{8}$	$\frac{1}{8}$	$\frac{1}{8}$	$\frac{1}{8}$

MY FRACTION WORD PROBLEM

TOPIC 7

Probability and Statistics

Name ____________________

Close Your Eyes

NO PEEKING!

Write the colors of the marbles (or cubes) in the first column. Then make a tally mark each time you select a color.

Color	Number of Times Picked

1. What color did you select most often?

____

2. What color did you select least often?

____

3. Which two colors did you select about the same number of times?

____

4. What color do you think you have the most of? Why?

____

____

____

____

____

IT'S VERY LIKELY, UNTIL YOU CLOSE YOUR EYES.

Choose the word or phrase from the word bank that best describes the likelihood of the event in each problem. Explain your answer.

WORD BANK				
Certain	Likely	Equally likely	Unlikely	Impossible

1. If these pieces of paper were put in a bag, what is the likelihood that you will pick a piece with the number 8 on it?

2. How does the likelihood of picking a 3 compare to the likelihood of picking a 4?

Name ____

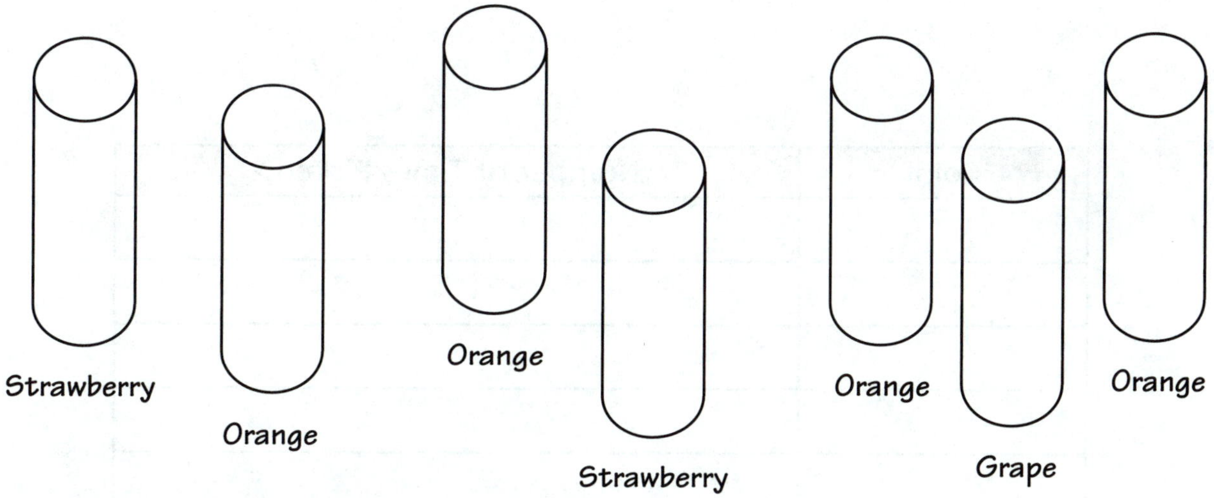

3. Tucker likes grape, strawberry, and orange Freezy Fruits. If Tucker closes his eyes and chooses one of the Freezy Fruits above, what is the likelihood he will select a flavor he likes?

4. What is the likelihood Tucker will select a grape Freezy Fruit?

5. If these cards were turned facedown and shuffled, what is the likelihood of your selecting an animal card?

TALLY HO!

Color	Number of Times Picked

Use the results of your experiment to answer the question. Explain your answer.

1. What color are you likely to pick from the bag?

____

2. What color are you unlikely to pick from the bag?

____

3. Which colors are equally likely to be picked?

____

4. What are you certain to pick?

____

5. What would be impossible to pick?

____

Name ____

HOME CONNECTION: HOW LIKELY IS THAT?

Dear Parent or Guardian:

Your child has been learning how to determine the likelihood of an event. Please conduct the likelihood experiment described below with your child.

- Fill a paper bag with at least 4 different colors of the same item, such as marbles.
- Tell your child what type of item (marbles, for example) is in the bag. But do not tell him or her how many different colors there are, or how many of each color there are.
- Be sure that one color represents more than half the items in the bag.
- Be sure that there is an equal number of two other colors in the bag.

After your child has done the experiment and answered the questions on the next page, tell him or her what the actual contents of the bag are. That is, tell what colors are in the bag and how many there are of each color.

You may then wish to switch roles. Have your child fill the bag, using the same rules as above. Then you can do the experiment and answer the questions.

Pick from the bag 30 times. Replace the item each time. Complete the chart.

Color	Number of Times Picked

Use the results of your experiment to answer the question. Explain your answer.

1. What color are you likely to pick from the bag?

2. What color are you unlikely to pick from the bag?

3. Which colors are equally likely to be picked?

4. What are you certain to pick from the bag?

5. What would be impossible to pick from the bag?

6. Write the actual contents of the bag. What colors are in the bag? How many of each color are there?

Name ______________________________

Spin It!

POINT IT OUT

Spinner 1

Spinner 2

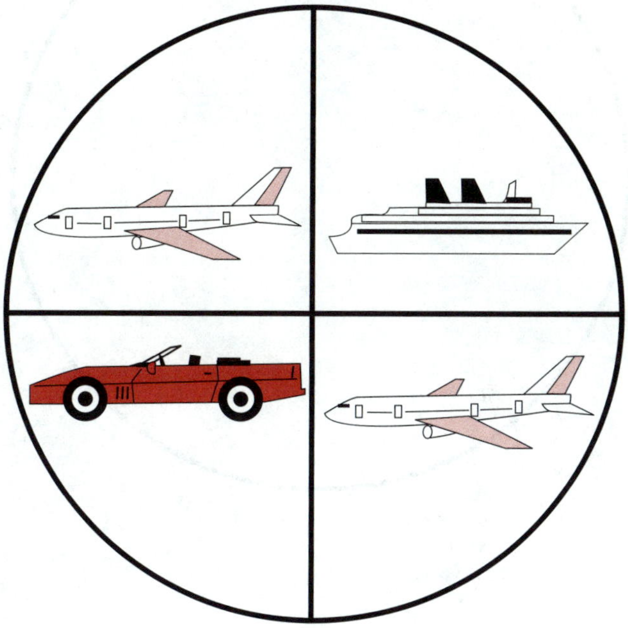

Spinner 3

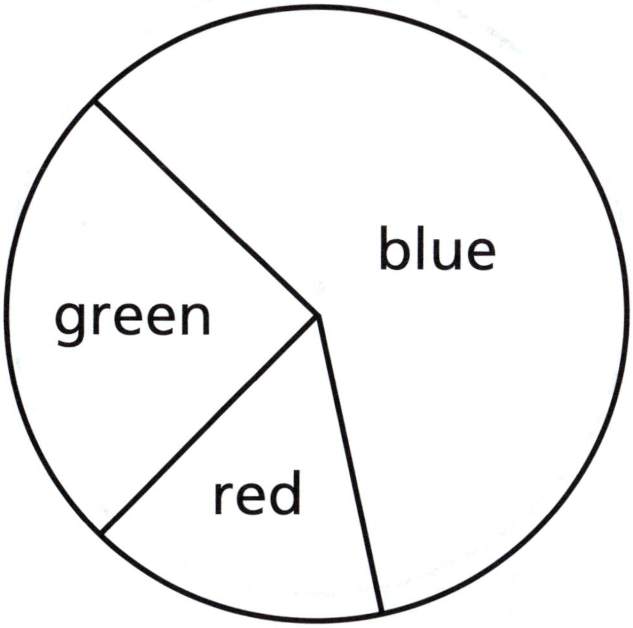

Spinner 4

SPIN AND WIN

Spinner A

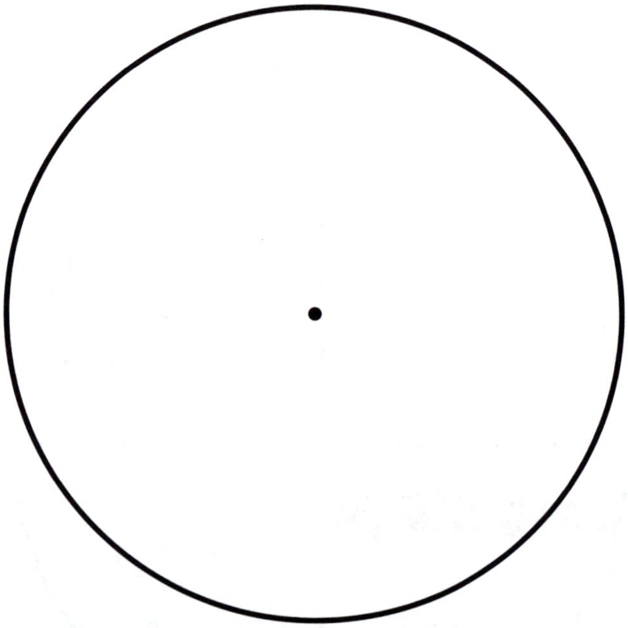

Spinner B

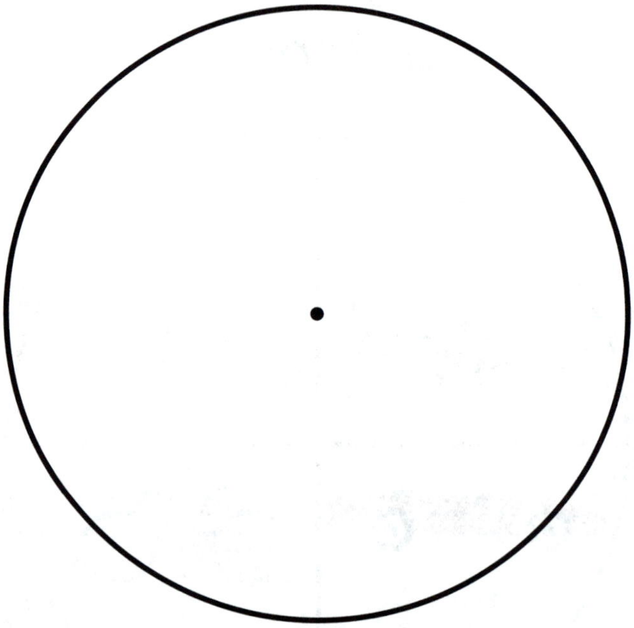

Spinner C

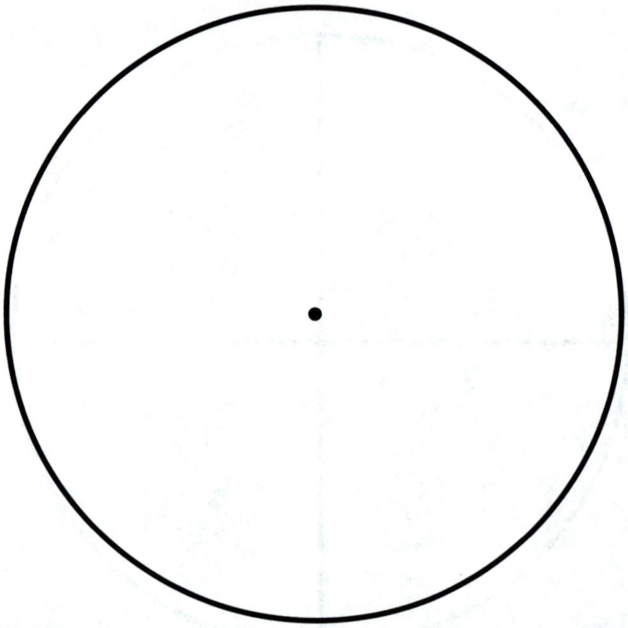

Spinner D

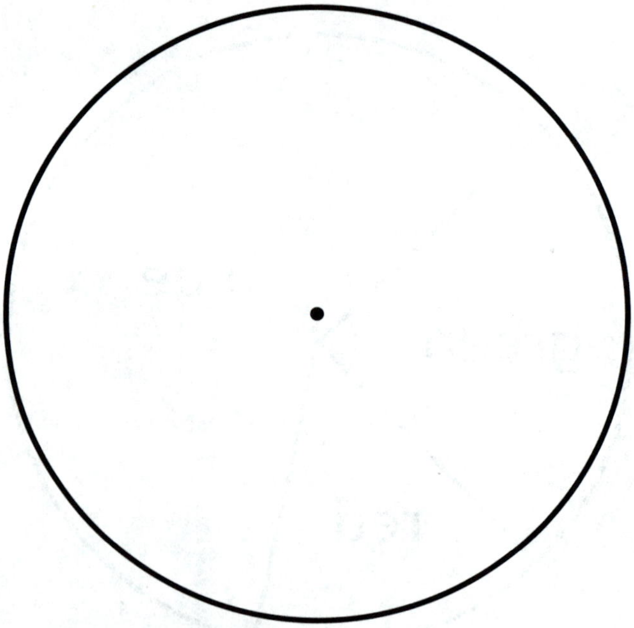

Name ______________________________

HOME CONNECTION: TWO-TONE EVENT

Dear Parent or Guardian:

Your child has been learning about probability, and conducting probability experiments with a spinner. On the other side of this page, he or she should design and color a spinner that has the probabilities listed. Have your child use a paper clip and pencil to show you how the spinner works.

Draw and color sections on the circle below to make a three-color spinner with the following probabilities:

- landing on the red or blue has a probability of $\frac{1}{2}$
- landing on blue has a probability of $\frac{1}{4}$
- landing on yellow has a probability of $\frac{1}{2}$

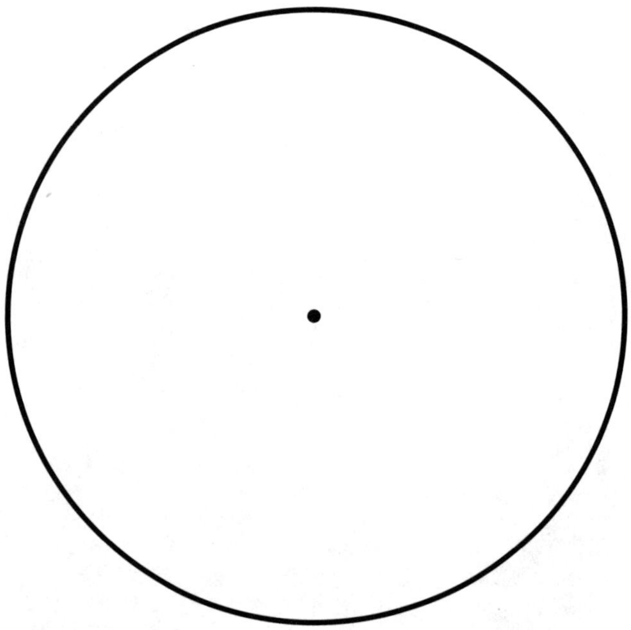

Name ______________________________

The Sundae Challenge

LET'S MAKE SUNDAES!

chocolate ice cream

vanilla ice cream

strawberry ice cream

nuts

jellybeans

cookie pieces

chocolate syrup

strawberry syrup

pineapple syrup

bowl

Name ____________________

SUNDAE TREES

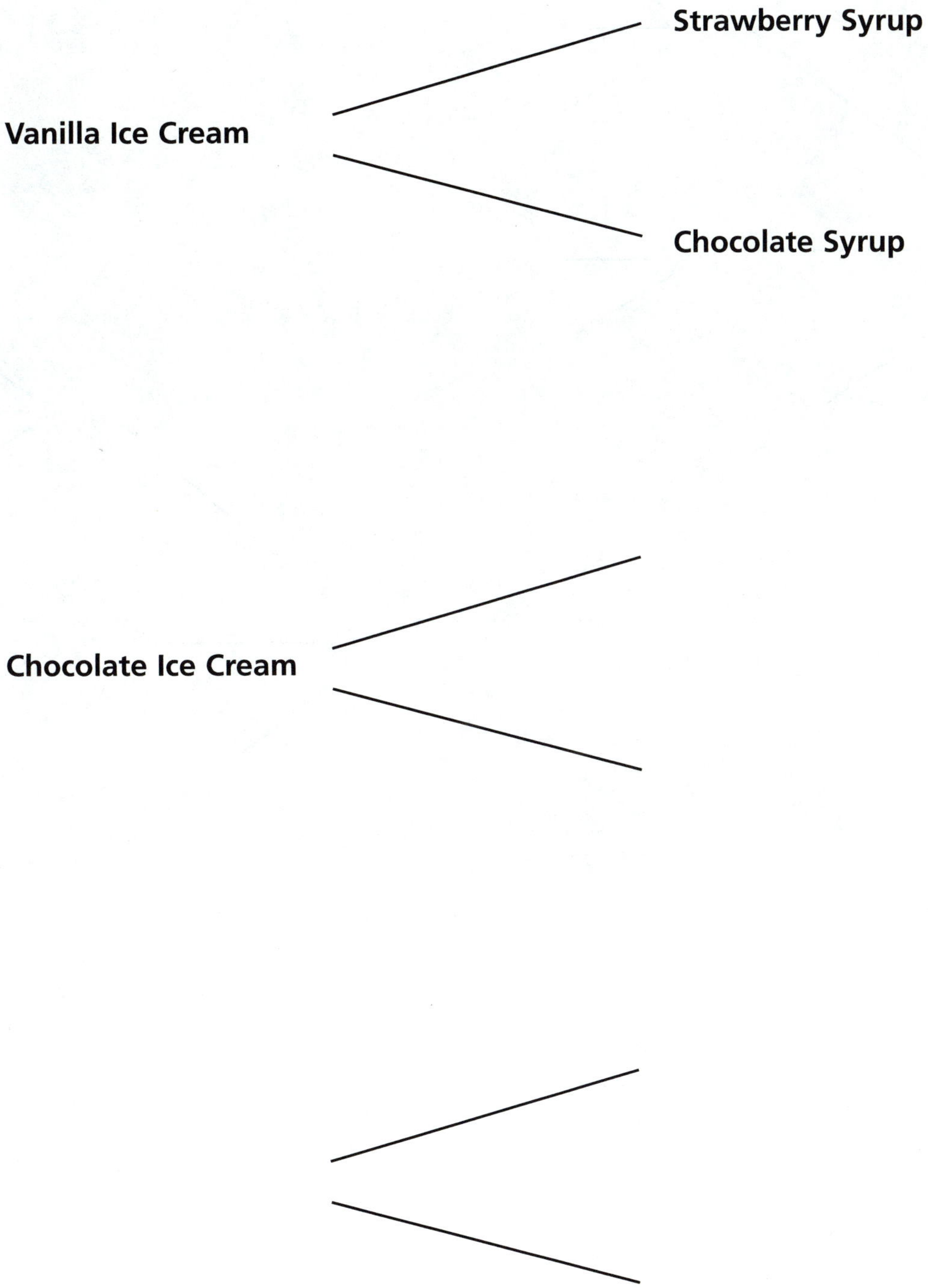

A FEAST OF SUNDAES

Use the tree diagrams to show all the different sundaes you can make with 3 kinds of ice cream, 3 kinds of toppings, and 3 kinds of syrup.

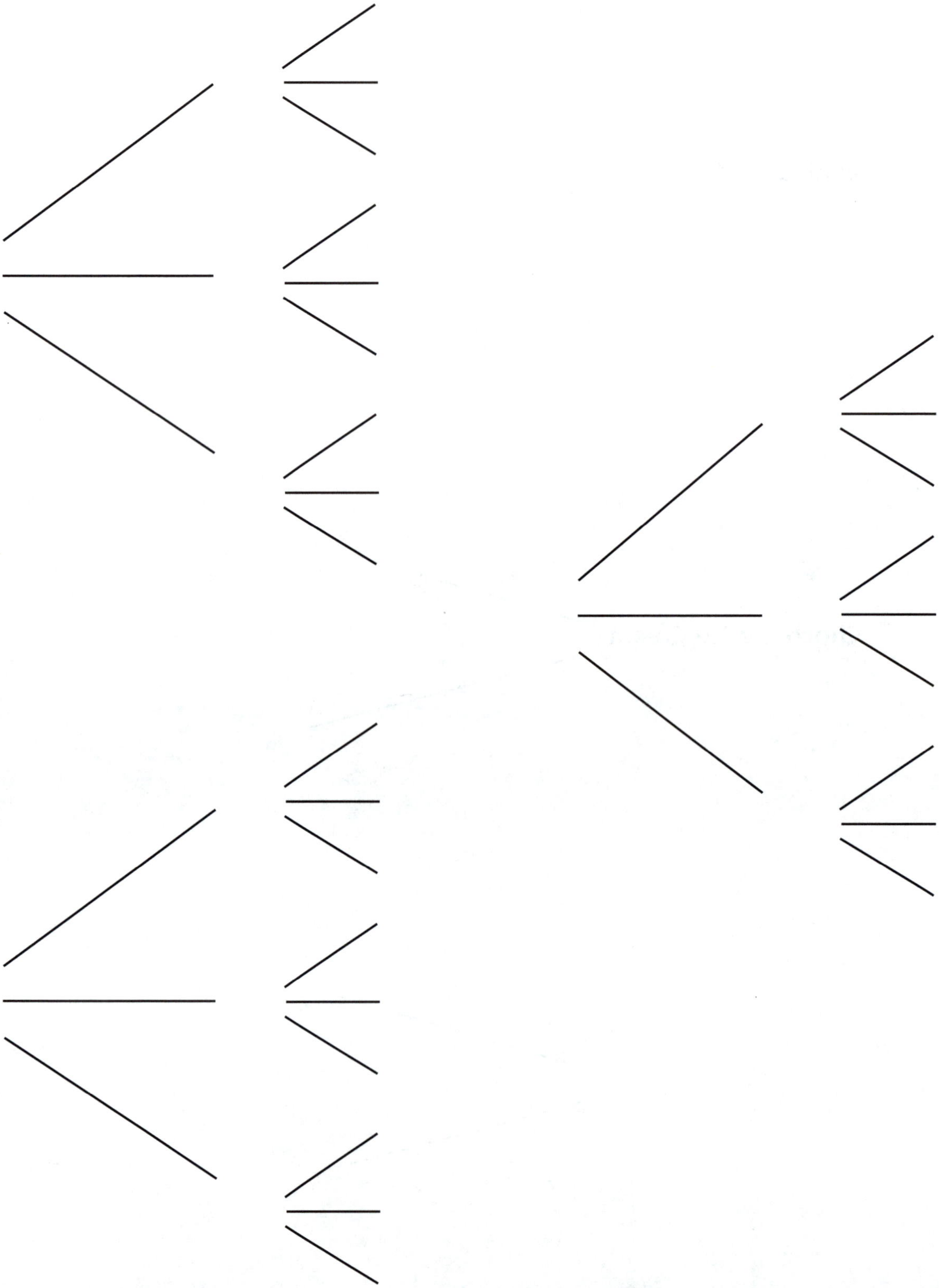

Name ____________________

HOME CONNECTION: SO MANY CHOICES

Dear Parent or Guardian:

Your child has been learning to use tree diagrams to show possible combinations of items. Please help your child solve the problems on this page and the next.

1. Cindy has two jackets (green and blue), two hats (checkered and striped), and three pairs of gloves (brown, black, and white). Use the tree diagram to show the different outfits that Cindy can choose from.

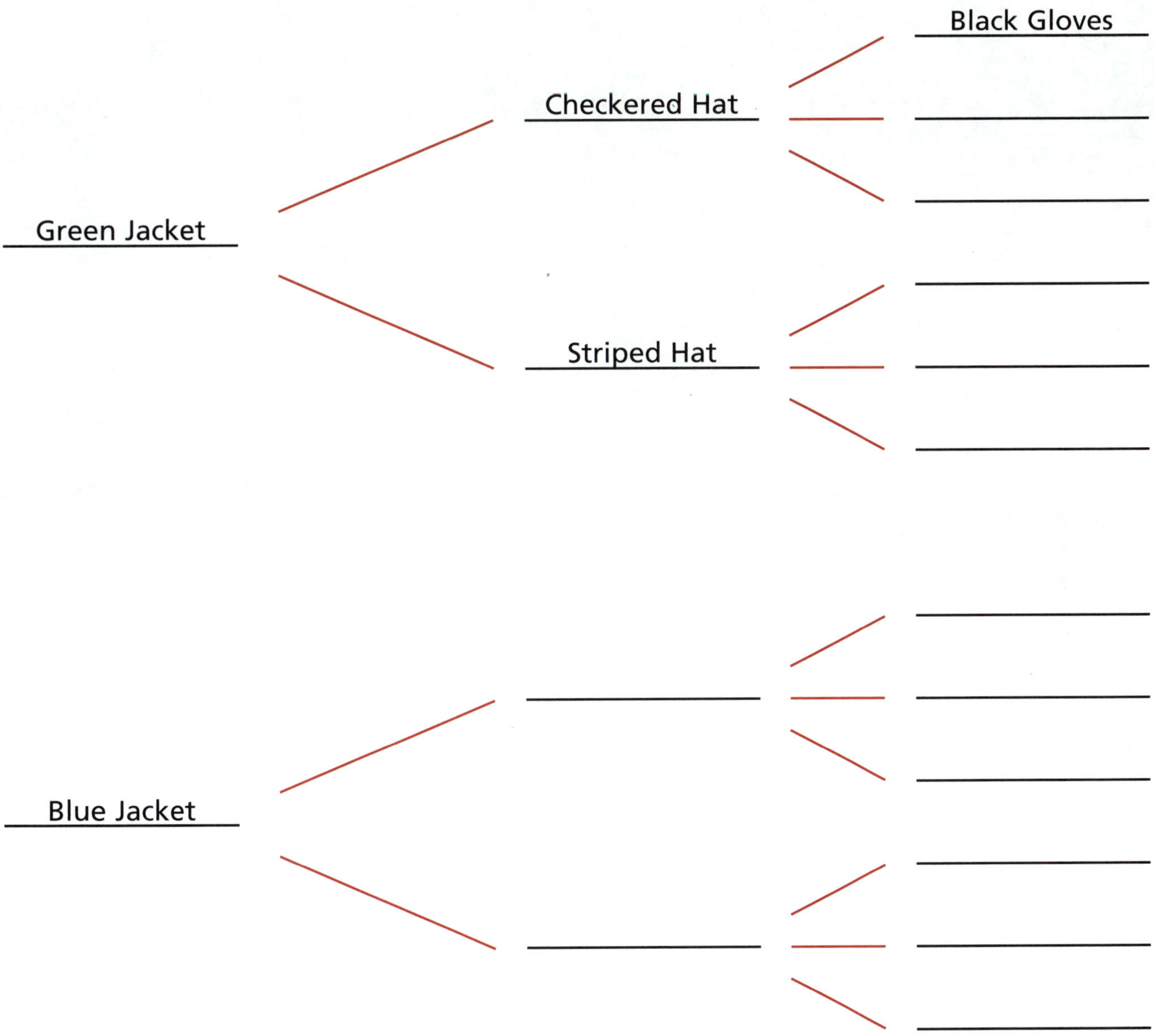

2. The deli offers sandwiches made on 3 types of bread (wheat, sourdough, and rye) with 2 types of cheeses (cheddar and Swiss) and 3 types of meat (roast beef, turkey, and ham). How many different sandwiches can you choose from, using 1 kind of bread, 1 kind of cheese, and 1 kind of meat? Make a tree diagram to help you solve the problem.